Greater Things

ENDORSEMENTS

"From flat-line to sunshine, this story takes you on an unbelievable heart-crossing journey."

Scott Pettit
Double Take

"Kristin is a strong, beautiful, and spirited individual and her story is deeply moving. I'm happy that everyone will get the chance to hear it."

Jonathan Larroquette
Comedy Podcast Host

"Plucked from her fun-loving, teenage existence, to getting tossed into a dark and difficulty reality after a brush with death, *Greater Things* is the story of Kristin Beale that you'll not soon forget. Captivating from the get-go, discover how Kristin and her family survived and thrived through hard work, courage, and an unflinching faith despite the paralyzing setback that landed her in a wheelchair. Forced to find a "new normal," she embraces her new life's path in a way that'll make you take stock of your own, reading as she fights adversity at every turn to find smiles, acceptance, purpose, and even shiny marathon medals along the way. THIS is what inspiration is all about. As a fellow paraplegic, Kristin's tale is one I'm deeply familiar with…and I still couldn't put it down. Neither will you. Believe what you hear – *Greater Things* is a triumphant must-read! Funny and sad, shocking and uplifting, heart-felt and familiar. This book has it all, folks!"

Michael Murphy
Motivational Speaker, Paralyzed Athlete, Writer at
MichaelMurphySpeaks.com

"Kristin writes with a winning combination of precision and heart. She has the amazing ability to describe the reality of her accident and her journey through almost innumerable therapies of all sorts. The sensory, the emotional, and the spiritual detail make her experience come to life. Greater Things captures the reality of what it means to be human. So if you are human, you also should read this book."

David Roche
Inspirational Humorist, LoveAtSecondSight.org

Greater Things

Kristin Beale

NEW YORK

NASHVILLE • MELBOURNE • VANCOUVER

Greater Things

Published in New York, New York, by Morgan James Publishing. Morgan James is a trademark of Morgan James, LLC. www.MorganJamesPublishing.com

The Morgan James Speakers Group can bring authors to your live event. For more information or to book an event visit The Morgan James Speakers Group at www.TheMorganJamesSpeakersGroup.com.

ISBN 9781683503675 paperback
ISBN 9781683503682 eBook
Library of Congress Control Number: 2016919321

Cover Design by:
Chris Treccani
www.3dogdesign.net

Interior Design by:
Chris Treccani
www.3dogdesign.net

In an effort to support local communities, raise awareness and funds, Morgan James Publishing donates a percentage of all book sales for the life of each book to Habitat for Humanity Peninsula and Greater Williamsburg.

Get involved today! Visit
www.MorganJamesBuilds.com

Thank you *to my family for being my best critics and supporting me through this whole process.*

Thank you *specifically to my sister, Jessica, who is both my best friend and my partner in crime. I love you more than you know.*

Thank you *to my editors and proofreaders for catching typos, correcting silly mistakes, and telling me when my jokes aren't funny.*

Thank you *to the community of people who supported, prayed for, and rooted for me since the beginning.*

Thank you *to everyone at Morgan James Publishing for being patient and professional with me and my book. You made my dream come true.*

Thank you, thank you, thank you.

CONTENTS

FOREWORD

Imagine yourself and your family cast into a scenario not of your choosing, that quickly evolves into a nightmare. A blind punch encased by death, loneliness, dismissiveness and solitude. You're new to this world because you can never imagine being part of it. No one can prepare you for what you are about to feel or experience because it is not a place anyone wants to go, nor a club anyone wants to join. Such is the story of Kristin Beale.

You've chosen to read this book for a couple of reasons. You have either heard of Kristin, observed her from afar and what she has accomplished to overcome that dark place where she found herself or, more importantly, you've been in a dark place yourself and want to know how to find the light. The purpose of the following pages is not limited to those that share the specific challenges she finds herself constantly overcoming. This is not a story about a mountain; it's about the climb.

I am Kristin's father. Being a father is by far one of my greatest responsibilities. It was easy in the beginning; little babies aren't too hard to please or manage. Then the stages came with maturity. That's hard enough, but throw in two girls that are two years apart. To my wife's credit, she always focused on the same message to them: Your sister is your best friend. I watched as they changed and grew into two wonderful people —strong-willed and determined, but always close. Most of us dads don't truly know how successful we are until the product of our efforts is put to the test. This test came with a vengeance.

Since 2005 when Kristin was injured, we have watched personal disappointment manifest in just about every channel imaginable. Cruelty in personal relationships (people known and not known), total lack of encouragement from medical professionals, gazing stares at her in a wheelchair, and an overall sense of "being in the way." Conversely and more importantly, we have observed an extension of grace (people known and not known), innocent conversation about her condition followed by encouragement, an overwhelming sense of support, and people getting OUT of the way. Kristin, at such a young age, has taught her family and those she touches more about forgiveness than most can comprehend.

If you're like most that have heard of or met Kristin, you will emote differently with every story in this book. It goes from shocking, to humorous, to sad, but in every story there's a message. It is consistent, which is why the title bears such great insight. You will live as she lives and truly understand there is nothing you cannot overcome. Her faith in and praise of a living God in all aspects of her life, good and bad, has been singularly the most compelling reason she is still here with us today.

The book was written in a format of several stories that chronicle Kristin's struggles, victories and insights. Kristin is not under any illusion that her plight is worse than others; actually, quite the opposite. To this day, she celebrates the anniversary of the day her world changed. While she was only inches from the end of her mortality, she will tell you that it changed her life, opened her eyes, and made her a warrior. If nothing else, you will be more cognizant that no matter who you meet, everyone is fighting some kind of battle. Her writing will give you the perspective to remember and appreciate that there is a way to deal with those battles. Whether you read it in one sitting or come back to it several times, it is timeless.

Throughout the book, you'll notice italicized passages that are excerpts of entries I made on Kristin's Caringbridge website, which is a blog site used by families to keep those concerned up to date on their loved ones' progress when struck down by accidents, deadly disease, physical tragedies, etc. They are included for a reason. Kristin's book is her perspective looking out, but those entries also give one of a parent looking in. Since the first day of her accident, I used the site to keep the rumor mill from getting out of control. Looking back, it was truly the best move made and, over the past 11 years, gave Kristin a perspective she has grown to appreciate.

And now….on to Greater Things.

Chris Beale
Richmond, Virginia

BAREFOOT MEMORIES

The sun was hot on my back as I stepped off the grass onto the dock. I walked along the weathered wood planks toward the water until I reached the bumpy fiberglass floor of Aubrey's Jet Ski. Warm water rushed around my feet and ankles while I situated myself behind Mark in the back seat. These are my last barefoot memories.

I have a collection of memories from the bottoms of my feet – some vivid, most faded. I replay them over and over in my head: soft carpet, new grass, cemented sidewalks, and the wet tile of the shower floor. I remember how it felt to slide on the bottom of the swimming pool and how it left the tips of my toes raw after every day of the summer. I remember feeling like my feet were going to fall off at my ankles on the 10th lap running around the field hockey field at my high school, and I'll never forget the sensation of a paint brush on my toenails when Mom took me and Jessica for pedicures.

Of all my barefoot memories, though, my favorite is this: walking on the hardwood floor. I remember how it pressed underneath my calloused skin. I remember the way it made me – and wherever I was walking – feel important. I remember the excitement of wearing socks and sliding around the foyer of my family's house, and I remember being able to sneak around late at night or early in the morning without waking everyone with my squeaks.

CHAPTER 1

Introduction

For my first year in high school and into the summer before my sophomore year, I was on top of the world. My grades were slightly above average, I was active on 3 competitive sports teams, and I got along well with my family. Freshman year had been the best year of my life, and summertime only exaggerated that. I had tan skin, an athletic body, and more friends than I could count on two hands. I was invincible.

The end of August came and Aubrey invited me to her house in Lake Gaston. I was less than one week shy of turning 15 years old and school started on Monday, so it was our last chance at summer. I've known Aubrey since we were kids in Sunday School, but we'd only just started hanging out outside of Sunday mornings.

"Mark is coming, too" she said. "I don't think you know him. And you remember Feild."

I recognized Mark from school, and I'd just met Feild on a church youth group trip a couple weeks before. Aubrey introduced us in the church parking lot and I liked him immediately after meeting. Feild is tall with light brown hair and a smile that's contagious. I remember positioning myself in the line loading onto the church van so that "natural" order would lead me to sit next to him. When my plan didn't work, I squished directly behind him and to the edge of the seat, balancing uncomfortably for the whole ride. I was trying to stay close as I could without appearing as captivated as I felt.

The day was a mix of roller coaster rides, hot dogs, and theme park games and, by the time we loaded on the bus to go home, I was crushing hard. Feild was easy to talk to and made me feel comfortable. He made me laugh and that's the biggest reason I liked him.

Now, one week later, I was invited to spend an entire weekend with him. I couldn't wait. A lot was riding on that trip. I bought a new bathing suit, packed my cutest summer clothes, and washed my hair. It was my chance to show off to Feild. He would realize our mutual attraction, ask me to be his girlfriend, happily ever after—or at least until homecoming.

Aubrey's lake house sat on a hill with a yard that led to a dock covered by a boathouse. I've lost most of the details from that weekend, but I remember climbing onto the roof and jumping into the water below. I remember hearing Feild's laugh before I hit the water and I remember how excited I felt when he smiled at me. I was on my best behavior, just hoping he would like me. I remember trying so hard.

On our last afternoon of the trip, Aubrey's Dad gave us permission to take out their two jet skis tied at the end of the dock: Feild driving Aubrey and Mark driving me. We chased each other around the lake and bounced across the waves with my arms tightly wrapped around Mark's waist. The only thing to slow us down was a No Wake Zone through an area where people were swimming.

As we pushed past the swimming area, Mark slowed our Jet Ski to a crawl before accelerating into the waves. I heard Feild and Aubrey's ski coming from behind us so I turned to look in what would be my last moments of consciousness. Their ski accelerated and slammed into us from behind, landing on top of us.

One second is all it took.

The impact of the collision forced Mark forward into the steering wheel and jerked me off the side into the water.

A group of people on a nearby boat saw everything. In seconds, they called the Coast Guard and were swimming toward our limp bodies in the water. I call them my angels. They were the first in a series of miracles that day.

Even though our crash was outside of the Coast Guard's regular route, a crew was close by. They were able to reach us in less than 5 minutes and call the rescue squad, also "coincidentally" nearby. Second miracle.

Mark and I were transported from the middle of Lake Gaston to a local medical center where Mark was declared dead on arrival. From there, I was airlifted to Pitt Memorial Hospital in Greenville, North Carolina where doctors induced a medical coma to prevent my body from going into shock from the trauma of my injuries. My parents were told I would not live. Aubrey and Feild were unhurt.

In the time it takes to tie your shoelaces, the happiest year of my life came to an abrupt halt. Everything I'd ever known was turned inside out.

My parents were out of town on vacation when they got the call. They raced home to Richmond to pick up my sister, Jessica, with my best friend Katie and her parents following closely behind. Everyone dropped what they were doing to be with me during the worst time in my life.

I don't have any memory of my time at Pitt, but I surprised everyone by staying alive. After a couple of weeks, the doctors told my family that I stood a greater chance of dying than surviving. Even so, one intern told my parents "she is the strongest I've ever seen."

My parents were given a more complete and numbing list of my injuries.

Kristin arrived at Pitt Memorial unconscious and by helicopter on the afternoon of the 28th. She suffered 2 collapsed lungs, lacerations in her spleen, kidney, and liver of a category 4 on a scale of 1 to 6 – 6 being the worst. Her brain was bruised with a closed head injury. Her blood pressure is extremely low and she is nonreactive to physical stimulation below her naval. Both lungs were bruised as well. Her T11 and T12 vertebrae are misaligned and cracked. She is on a respirator, not breathing on her own. There was internal bleeding in her brain and lower abdomen. Officially, her injuries are as follows:

1. *Multi Trauma*
2. *Traumatic brain injury with subarachnoid hemorrhage*
3. *Spinal cord injury with paraplegia*
4. *Multiple rib fractures, T8 through L2*
5. *Left hemothorax*
6. *Grade 4 liver lacerations*
7. *Multiple grade 1 splenic lacerations*
8. *Mediastinal hematoma*
9. *Right adrenal hematoma*

Immediately after the accident she also suffered pneumomediastinum, rhabdomyolysis, acute blood loss, shocked bowel, blunt cardiac injury, large retroperitoneal hematoma, left corneal abrasions, respiratory failure, and pericardial effusion with tamponade.

The first days after my accident were critical for my diagnosis. Also, as you can imagine, the most stressful and heartbreaking for my loved ones.

Concern about her heart and blood around her heart result in an Echocardiogram and "Swan" to test its function. Concern about her renal gland producing enough steroids results in more fluids and steroids given to help stabilize her body. A CAT scan shows blood in her brain. However, it does not seem worse than original scan…this is good news. Today is an important day in that 48 hours is when injuries look the worst. It appears that the worst has already occurred and there is no swelling in her brain. All other functions are improving, but not as quickly as we expected. Sedation and pain medicine is reduced with the expectation that she will start to awaken, but to no avail.

After 3 days of being "knocked out" from drugs, my doctors started to get a fuzzy, but still more clear, idea of my outcome. They told my parents they are "very certain" that I'll be paralyzed from the waist down. I don't know how my parents reacted to that news and it hurts my heart to have to imagine it. But I was still alive. Most importantly, I was alive.

Around 6:00pm, she moves. She pulls her arm away from a restrictive belt and touches her breathing tube, but doesn't jerk on it. Very good news. Shortly thereafter, the nurse says "if you can hear me, give me thumbs up". Kristin responds with a tiny little thumbs up! She begins to strongly protest the belts on her and pushes very hard (strong girl). The nurse tells her to calm down and grab Elliot's trunk. Elliot is her stuffed elephant she's had since age 5 and goes EVERYWHERE with her. Kristin "feels around" until she finds the trunk and squeezes it tight. This is phenomenal as she has 1) followed a command and 2) knows who Elliot is. She is then sedated to keep her at rest and calm.

My family and few close friends stayed beside me at the hospital the whole time. I was still in bed, unconscious, and highly medicated, but I was fighting. I was fighting for the moments that I could give my parents something, anything, to let them know I was still there. But life went on. The world was moving on without me.

Jessica celebrated her 17ᵗʰ birthday tonight, complete with a cake and presents from well-wishers and family. She has been the rock of our family through this whole ordeal. Jessica and Kristin are best friends and Jessica's faith has been unyielding.

I thought of Kristin and Jessica all day yesterday. Sometimes, there are days when my mind is preoccupied with thoughts of where they started up to where they are now. So many memories of how they laughed uncontrollably at stupid little jokes, some of which they still tell. When they were kids and Jessica paused from her playtime to run up and kiss Kristin (still an infant in her baby rocker chair) on the cheek. Jessica's fat little arms hugging her baby sister and sometimes simply sitting beside her just to hold her tiny hand. Jessica's ability to make Kristin simply look at her and smile. Rhonda always told them that in life there would no better friend than each other. We always thought it fell on deaf ears because they would bicker so much. What we didn't know is that more often than not, they were partners in schemes around Mom and Dad. I think the phrase is "thick as thieves", but not in the literal sense.

Then came August 28th. I go back to one of the darkest hours in our family...all very heart wrenching. The uncertainty, the waiting, being displaced from each other when we found out, Jessica at home alone, us being 2.5 hours from home and 5 hours from Pitt County hospital, picking up Jessica in Mechanicsville for the drive to Pitt, the tears that flowed as we stood in the Walmart parking lot; the three of us in a "group hug," Kristin being airlifted as we drove to Pitt, the confusion at the hospital in trying to find her and, of course, when we saw her in critical condition fighting for her life. The look on Jessica's face as she saw her baby sister and best friend for 15 years, so helpless and broken. I've said this before, but Jessica's strength and optimism throughout those painful days in North Carolina was God sending us support. Looking back, it seems superhuman.

And, now, today....still bickering at times, but more than not, they still look at each other, laugh.....look at Rhonda and me, and then laugh harder. There's an inseparable bond there that I could only hope to understand. I don't dare encroach by asking "what's so funny?"

We are surely blessed by not only having two daughters, but by them being so close and loving each other so much.

Slowly, very slowly, I started to come back. The first indicator was my efforts to free myself from a respirator tube in my mouth. I was very athletic before my accident, remember, so I put up a good fight. But the hospital has sedation meds so I lost that battle as quick as a needle poke.

My little girls is alive, but there are still things to deal with. Her spinal cord in not severed, but the Trauma Chief does think it's damaged. Again, her spine just a picture on a screen right now. Still no movement from her legs.

When I was speaking with the doctor by her side, her heart rate increased quite a bit as she could hear my voice. We had to step outside to continue the conversation. She is due to have back surgery after she is stabilized, which we hope will be this weekend. We will continue to try and raise her consciousness periodically to see if we can get her to respond to pain in her lower body.

A bigger question than sensation and movement lost from my spinal cord injury was the effects of my traumatic brain injury. That was the real panic.

The amount of brain injury is undetermined. Apparently, the areas of the brain that are bruised would affect memory, vision, and some learning ability. Her right pupil is inconsistent with her left pupil. Physically, she continues to be strong...heartrate is steady, blood pressure is good, and she is initiating breathing on her own. She is still hooked up to a respirator until she can breathe independently. Every time Kristin goes through a mouth cleaning, she grabs Elliott's trunk and calms down.

Like I said, life went on. I "celebrated" my 15th birthday, Jessica started her senior year of high school, and all of my friends went on without me. I was missing everything and I didn't even know it.

My body was very hard at work, though. I was coming back.

Kristin has been bathed (she is bathed twice daily) and her hair brushed and styled a little. We can see her face without all the plumbing now. I must tell you that she is beautiful. Her resting heart rate is now around 80, versus 120, and her breathing is regular.

Right after surgery we went in to visit but, after about 15 minutes, we were asked to leave due to a shift change. Before I left I spoke to her softly and told her I would be returning soon. She gently squeezed my hand…a Living Moment. I told her "Kristin if you can hear me, squeeze my hand." She squeezed harder. The doctor said "Ask her to let go." This is to see if it was just a reflex or is she was following commands. She let go! I did the squeeze and release one more time and she did it on command.

Everyone take a moment…stop praying and start praising.

It breaks my heart to see the desperation and pain everyone was feeling because of me. It absolutely fills my heart, though, to see the sacrifice and love from the people around me during that time. My family is incredible and the ICU team at Pitt Memorial Hospital was outstanding.

The nurses have allowed Rhonda to spend the night in her room every night so far, which is against their "official policy." I've tried to drag her out, but anyone who knows Rhonda can attest that I'm wasting my time. She's as stubborn as a mule (that's a good thing).

Kristin continues to be motionless below her naval, but is very strong from the waist up. Please keep praying that her legs will move very soon.

Even with the good news and improvements I was making, I cannot fathom the pain my family went through. I feel guilty because, in a way, I'm responsible for all of that. But I just have to remind myself that it's not my fault. It's not my fault.

Pray for Rhonda. Although she says "I'm doing fine," she has spent every single night in Kristin's room watching her breathe...just like we did when she was born. You parents know what I mean. I find that literally hours have gone by and all I've done is watch her breathe and look at her monitors while she lays there motionless. I've whispered in her ears so many times for her to pray for her own healing. Her prayers along with what seems like thousands of prayers from you guys, is making miracles happen daily. She is trying so hard to come back to us.

I was getting better and my body was healing. Here's the key: faith. My faith in God leading up to the moment of my accident was strong, sure, but my tragedy made it real. My accident made it applicable.

We were able to get Kristin's bible from the house this past Friday. I opened it for a moment. I must share with you that Kristin absolutely loves God. It is obvious that she has been studying the bible in her spare time because her notes and favorite verses are marked throughout. I know that she is praying for her healing. I told her today that she's in the hospital and doing well. I am most certain she doesn't know why she's here and I pray she doesn't remember the incident just yet.

A little over 2 weeks after my accident, I really started to wake up. My dad tells a story of me throwing stuffed animals at him from my hospital bed, consistently responding to commands, and even some rebounding personality.

Right after I returned to the hospital from writing the last entry, I was blessed with a Living Moment again. I was talking to Kristin and trying to make her laugh – which really only can qualify if I can furrow her brow. After making several faces and hitting her with some of my best material, she had not done much more than look at me with that "what a dork" look on her face. I'm used to this as I many times get the same look at neighborhood events. So, I resorted to a little more complicated tactic and simply asked her to smile at me. Dramatic pause and then…Cha Ching! She smiled at me and Rhonda witnessed it. Confirmed and logged.

After spending about one month at Pitt, I was moved to MCV's Intensive Care Unit in my hometown of Richmond, Virginia. My body was still extremely frail and recovery still a question. I was coming back, though.

We have no doubt that the move was the correct one. The reason is not necessarily because MCV is closer to home, but that is a large benefit. The reason is primarily because we have so many networked friends in the medical industry from top to bottom: nurses, neurologists, surgeons, physical therapists, etc. Everyone who knows us and can be involved in Kristin's care at MCV has jumped through hoops to check on her and us. We are blessed with that comfort. God put them here for us and they are instrumental in our journey.

The first few days at MCV were laced with small, but significant, victories of my consciousness. There was still an elephant in the room, though: my legs. And I'm not talking about my stuffed animal Elliott, but rather the unconfirmed fate of my mobility. As time passed and the more serious concerns of my survival were eliminated, that elephant went from just standing in the room, to standing on our heads.

I must admit, today Kristin seems kind of sad. She has come around a bit more and for only minutes at a time, but she is now asking questions about her legs. She was told by a nurse that just because they aren't moving now doesn't mean they'll never move. It will take time. When she heard this,

Kristin's eyes filled up with tears and she went back to sleep. I think in her mind, all she heard was "they aren't moving now." In an active 15 year old's mind, she wants to jump up and walk out and play field hockey again.

Starting at Pitt and lasting to MCV, I survived beyond doctors' initial bleak predictions. Their forecasting to my parents got a little more specific. I would live, they said, but I would be unable to speak, swallow, feel or move below my injury. Oh, and one more thing: I'd have the mental capacity of a ladybug.

I continued to prove my doctors wrong when I returned to consciousness in October, could form complete sentences, and function as a close-to-normal teenager. The miracles continue.

Kristin is alive, can express herself, recognize her family and friends, can brush her own teeth, can still make people laugh, can spell, and has memory. All of these things were not probable on August 28th. She was not slated to live but, after staring down the Grim Reaper, she kept on continuing to improve. She has a long road ahead of her. From this point forward, we all have to continue to pray that we beat the odds of paralysis that seem to be mounting against her. Her mobility is at serious risk.

If you have a child, hug them tight for a long time and think about Kristin. Never forget that warm sensation of dependency. Tell them you love them every day. Right now, that is what is giving Kristin the strength to fight.

Staying alive and having my mind were the biggest priorities, of course. But I still have a hill to climb. It was fun to pass all those other milestones but, to this day, I continue to work to undo the last item on their list: walk. But I won't skip ahead.

Again, in mid-September, I was moved. My progress in recovery meant that I could be [heavily sedated and] transported from MCV's Trauma Center to Children's Hospital's Acute Care Unit. I was allowed to move only because I was able to breathe mostly on my own, meaning

I was less dependent on the trachea. That was exciting enough news by itself, but I was able to give a little bit more than that.

> *Kristin never ceases to amaze me. After we got her settled down in her new bed, Rhonda put Kristin's iPod into some speakers so she could listen to her favorite music. Kristin was coming around pretty quickly, but she was still a tiny bit out of it. Her short term memory loss is still in full swing.*
>
> *One of her favorite bands is David Crowder Band – a Christian music band. It was one of those moments where she and I were simply looking at each other. I do this whenever I can because it feels like she's trying to tell me something.*
>
> *She raised her hand with two fingers up. At first I thought she was pointing at something like the light on the ceiling. She looked at me and raised her hand even higher, still with two fingers up. I brought out the communication board. What she spelled made my heart leap. She pointed out G...O...D. She was raising her arm to God. Kristin was praising God. In her condition, she was saying "Ain't God great?"*

I wish I could say that the days following were filled with beautiful moments like those and my full cooperation. But nothing is that easy, am I right? Not only was I fighting my injuries to stay alive, but I was also fighting my machines and anything that was in my hospital bed's reach. I was a fighter.

> *Kristin was wide awake ALL night. This would not ordinarily be a problem because she's equipped with arm restraints around both wrists to preclude pulling out her strings. But when Bionic Woman is restrained, it might as well be Scotch tape holding her down. After a couple of adjustments to make her more confined, 2 shots of sedative medicine and 1 shot of Tylenol, she still had the power to break the arm bands...twice. Aside from a Kung Fu grip, she's got guns – especially on the left arm. so what's the solution? You guessed it. I stood beside her and held her hand all night. And, of course, it was a battle every time she wanted to pull her strings.*

Very tiring. At around 7:00 she went to sleep and has been hard to revive all day. That's OK because it's her last day of rest before her extensive rehab schedule starting tomorrow. Kristin is a tiger when she's awake.

My memory was still erasing itself every 10 minutes, but my mind was coming back to me. Again, very slowly. I gave my parents some moments to keep them going. They were rare, yes, but I had to give them something. They needed something to hold onto.

Today Kristin received a neat tool. It's basically a keyboard with a one line display. She can type her messages into it, versus spelling them out on her communication board. It's faster and more fun for her. It will also speak the words you type. Two things on that…

When she was being sat up on her bedside, the keyboard was within reach. She reached over and typed "OW" and hit Speak. She then told us that her back was hurting. We tend to forget she had back fusion surgery about 2 weeks ago, which is not a long time.

Another doctor was asking her questions that were general in nature like her age, what city she is in, what state, etc. She then asked her "Do you know where you are?" We were expecting her to say "in a hospital," but no. Smarty-Pants types out "in a room." She's a joker.

My parents expressed (through those journal entries) their sadness and dread for the inevitable of me "waking up" and asking what happened to me and why I was in the hospital. My mom and dad are two incredibly strong people and, again, I feel guilty and responsible for the pain they were feeling. But it's not my fault. It's not my fault.

Her right side continues to improve gradually but still no movement from her legs. At some point soon, Kristin will begin to ask questions. She is no longer on any type of sedation drugs. This phase will be a very sad time as we do not believe she remembers the accident. Our pain has not diminished, but it will be worsened to witness her realizing the painful truth for the first time while we, simultaneously, will have to relive it all over again. At some point we progressed in our grieving of mentally picturing the accident, to focusing on Kristin's survival and progress. To go into replay mode seems unfair, but she needs to know if she asks. We anticipate these questions to begin sometime later this week. She is moving on from a physical perspective, but the worst thing would be for her emotional situation to set her back. Please pray that we receive the guidance and emotional fortitude to deal with her questions.

These are all moments and memories that my short term memory loss took from me. It's kind of weird to read these journal entries that detail things I said and did, and have no recollection of any of it. Those early days I spent in the Acute Care Unit of Children's Hospital aren't necessarily memories I want, though, so it's okay.

Remember I said that the doctors and nurses at all the hospitals I stayed in were outstanding. Speech Therapy showed me how to guide my lips to say words, regardless of no sound coming from my mouth. When I started doing that and my parents mastered the art of comprehending my lip movements, I was finally able to express myself. The trachea in my throat prohibited me from being able to speak like a normal person so, aside from typing words into a talking box, I was a mute. But now, finally, I could express myself. More specifically, I could express some frustration. My brain injury was still in full swing at that point, though. Please excuse my rude behavior. It's kind of funny.

Another erratic night of on and off sleep. I think the drugs she's given to put her to sleep have an adverse effect on her. She didn't recognize me and said I was "a man off the street" when I asked her who I am. Later, she came around and recognized me. Hospital room delirium, I suppose. She told me she was mad at me because "I hired a group of idiots" to take care of her. She obviously doesn't like being poked, prodded and forced to go to therapy. My explanations of how they are here to help were surely wasted in her state of mind. God bless this little girl in her journey back to us.

I passed my digestion test "with flying colors" and my trachea was reconstructed so I could speak at a normal volume. The same day I had the trachea reduction and as soon as I was able, I had questions. I knew my body was broken and I could see that my life was turned inside out, but I still didn't know why. What happened to me?

She has now asked that she be given the details of her accident. Tomorrow is our day to explain what put her in this condition. We will have a psychologist and chaplain on hand to help us in dealing with her response. As I said before, this is something that Rhonda and I do not want to do, but know that she deserves to know the truth. I ask that you pray that God will give us wisdom and emotional fortitude to be able to speak to her about this horrible situation.

I don't remember the conversation and it wasn't documented in this journal. By this time I was comprehending and responding to people and conversations around me, so I can assume that it was very hard for everyone. This is another memory I'm not upset about losing. There's no doubt that I comprehended my situation at that time, though.

Kristin mostly rested today. I think her therapy sessions are tough on her, so the weekend rest periods are beneficial. Her visits with friends were very good and I saw lots of smiles. At one point, however, I noticed a small tear rolling down. When I asked her why, she said "I want to run."

This makes me very sad. There's a reason that God has not healed that part of her and I may not know while I'm alive, but I'm faithful that it's all part of His plan for her. Good will come out of whatever the outcome is. Perhaps the "BIG" event will come soon and we'll see those legs move. Pray without ceasing.

Tomorrow is a special day for Kristin. Jessica will be coming to the hospital early in the morning to be with her during morning therapy sessions. Kristin is visibly excited with the news. Anything that lifts her spirits is so refreshing.

My mind was coming back, meaning my arms weren't tied down with pesky arm restraints anymore. I was getting there: I could whisper words, get out of bed, and express myself more like real people. In one of his journal entries from early October, Dad recorded a time that he and Jessica came into my hospital room "to see an alert, smiling, and beautiful little girl sitting up in bed." By that time I was able to hold both of my eyes wide open and maintain a weak, but still genuine, smile on my face.

Rhonda said she was asking for me all day. That was all I needed to hear. Her therapy sessions went very well today. She sat up for 4.5 minutes on her own (balancing). She is beginning to learn to transfer herself and she was very talkative. Kristin said she was in a good mood today. That is a wonderful thing to hear.

Things were starting to run smoothly for me – as smoothly as they can run from an inpatient ward of a hospital. I was reaching goals in therapy, I could sit upright in a chair for close to 5 minutes at a time, and I had a steady flow of people coming to visit me every day. Being stuck in a hospital was still the worst thing, but I was making it work. At least until they figured out my tricks.

Our weekly doctor's meeting went well as we heard good reports from all the therapists. We are now ratcheting her up to the next level…Tough Love. The therapists have as much as told us that they suspect Kristin has been using that "I'm nauseous, I hurt, I'm in pain, etc." to get out of working out like she should. And for the most part they've gone easier on her. But now it's going to be different. We all agreed that it's time for the tough love.

So here's the funny part. I went back to Kristin's room after the meeting to tell her how it went. When I relayed to her what I had heard she always seems nauseous during therapies, she said "They believe me when I say I'm nauseous, but I'm really not. I just do that so they'll let me stop working. But that's our secret, OK?" I had to laugh. I told her "You're SO busted.

*They're on to you and they've decided to kick it up a notch. You're going to be working your butt off and they won't stop when you complain anymore."
Kristin says "REALLY? No. SOME of them will still believe me, so I'll keep doing it." At that point Rhonda walked in and I told her what Kristin said. Rhonda said "KRISTIN! I've been taking up for you when you said that. You tricked me!" Kristin said "It's OK, Mom. I can still say it and you can lie. We can lie together!" We all had a good laugh at how clever she's been. Yep, I think my girl is coming back a little at a time.*

Life went on. While I laid in a bed at the hospital, my classmates and friends were getting their hair done, dressing up in beautiful dresses, meeting their dates to take pictures, and going to the Homecoming dance at my high school. It seems like a no-big-deal kind of event to be missing, but not being able to go to the dance with my friends meant more than just not going to a dance. It meant that I was an outcast. It meant that people were having fun without me. Although it wasn't likely, it meant me missing the opportunity to be asked on a date with a cute boy from my class. It hurt.

She never said anything, but I think I can read Kristin pretty well. Not being part of the Homecoming activities was sad. All I could think about was her if she could walk and how pretty she would look in a dress with that big smile of hers. When she went to prom last year she looked beautiful, but also possessed that little girl look in her eyes. It was an "I love my life" look that I'll never forget. What I see in her eyes now is "I want my life back, but I don't know if I can do this." No matter how much we tell her she can, she has to believe it herself.

And I do believe it. I eventually believed it, but he was right. I struggled with that a lot at first.

One month after our initial conversation about my accident, Dad and I talked about it again. Not surprisingly, my short term memory loss robbed me of the memory of our first conversation and, I realize as I read these journal entries, this second conversation was also erased in my memory. Anyway, here's round two.

> *Tonight, the opportunity came to discuss the accident in finite detail. When I say that, I mean it literally. She wanted to know not only dates, but names of people, minute by minute details, who did what and when, etc.*
>
> *She thought she was on the Jet Ski by herself. When I told her the whole story, she was very upset and understandably so. I took a very long time to discuss this with her. We talked about so many things. It will be a conversation that I will cherish for the rest of my life and will be unforgettable. Kristin is truly a gift to us. She is now aware of the death of Mark Brennan.*
>
> *I told her brief stories about the guest entries on this website and how many people have said they have a closer walk with God now. She said, "So it's a good thing that people are closer to God now because of what happened to me. That's good!" I don't think there's a selfish bone in her body. Our conversation drifted back and forth about how God has used this situation for good even though it seems so painful. ALL of her responses were geared toward being an instrument for God. She is incredible.*

After two months spent in the hospital, my consciousness returned to me in flashes – much like flipping through the photo album of a stranger. My short term memory loss finally started to fade in mid-October of the same year. It was a gradual and extremely tedious process that required a lot of patience from my family and friends that surrounded me. At that point in my life, I had a lot of friends to surround me.

Every day of the week from the time of my accident until discharge from the hospital, I had people wanting to visit me so often that they had to be limited to 2-3 per day to avoid overstimulation of my brain. When my memory was still fleeting, Mom took a picture of every visitor that came. She posted the pictures on the walls surrounding my hospital bed so I could always be reminded of the people who loved me, whether I remembered their visit or not. In most cases that's all they were: pictures. My memory was weak and in recovery for years after my accident.

I have few memories of my time in the hospital and even fewer memories of the month before my memory started coming back in October. There are a few, though. I clearly remember a Speech Therapy session with my therapist who I don't remember the name of. I remember her fingers pressing on the top of my tongue and her telling me to resist movement and push them off. She did the same thing from every angle and for every direction of my tongue. I was told those exercises were meant to strengthen my muscles, but I remember just thinking it was gross.

I have another misplaced but perfectly clear memory from that same therapist on a day before my memory came back to me. I remember sitting in the hospital's black and orange loaner wheelchair with its shoulder-high backrest, anti-tipping bars on the back, and clothing guards on either sides of my thighs. I remember sitting under the wooden table pressed against the back wall of the room and my therapist telling me to scream as loud as I could. In my mind I remember panicking and I remember hesitating for what felt like several minutes before following orders. The Speech Therapy room sat at the end of a runway of administrative offices and a Physical Therapy gym full of other patients – not the place for an outside voice. My memory gets blurred but I remember finally screaming and not at all expecting the result: it was a whisper. I remember my surprise and pushing my voice out hard as I could, to no avail.

My mind can still take me back to that hospital bed better than any other experience in the hospital, probably because it's where I spent most of my time. I remember the hard cot positioned next to a window leading into the cold, sterile hallway of the inpatient ward. Even though the curtains were always down, the light and the chaos found a way into my room and never left. The mattress wasn't comfortable, but it wasn't uncomfortable either. It was squishy and uneven, but it felt like the only place in the hospital building that I was happy. The pillows I laid on felt like water balloons, and not in a good way. A television hung on the wall directly in front of me and played droning daytime television until Mom and I couldn't stand it anymore. I spent a lot of time in that bed. Miserable as it was, laying down was as good as my life was going to get in that place.

To this day, more than 10 years later, I'm haunted by memories of my feeding tube and trachea. By the time I returned to consciousness I was already eating and breathing on my own, so I don't have memory from when I was still dependent on them – my memories begin when I had "place holders." They were shortened, plastic tubes that stuck into my body to fill openings in my stomach and throat where the feeding and breathing machines used to be. They just looked like large, plastic castles sitting 2-3 inches off the surface of my skin. My doctors were gradually shrinking them in size to help my body heal and close, leaving 2 heavy scars in their wake.

Those plastic castles sticking out of my body were always in the way: when I took a bath, when I lay in bed, pulled a shirt over my head, anything I did. I remember a crust that would form, again and again, between my skin and the plastic. My skin was extra sensitive around it but I remember scraping the crust off with my fingernails anyway. It was a little bit painful but I couldn't resist. It was like a hangnail that kept snagging, and snagging, and snagging.

Then my memory blacks out.

My short term memory loss erased memory of the weekend of my accident, those first months after, and the first moments I realized that I'm paralyzed. I'm not sure I want those memories. By the time my mind started coming back to me, I was already relatively deep into my rehabilitation and had too many things to do and to distract me. Because of that, I missed out on the sadness and lamentation that's expected in a situation like mine. Energy I would have used to regret or pity my situation is the same energy I need for rehabilitation of not only my body, but also my mind.

Because of the attention from the media and my community put on my accident, I felt tremendous pressure from an audience expecting what felt like near perfection. That meant I wasn't given the time to grieve and/or feel bad for myself because I had too much to do and too much to live up to. As soon as I was let free from the hospital I kept my mind and body as occupied as I could; I didn't give my inabilities the chance to settle in. I'm confident that played an important role in my acceptance and healing after the accident.

My journey began in Carlsbad, California two weeks after I was discharged from Children's Hospital in December, and I suspect will continue for the rest of my life – long after I'm able to walk. California is home to Project Walk, where I started with an intensive rehabilitation routine, continued until I got home to Richmond, and in numerous visits around the country over the years.

In one second I went from a confident teenager on top of the world and with no clear direction, to a struggling young adult with an unsolicited purpose to better myself and use my story as testimony to others. I was robbed of the opportunity to mature with my peers, and instead expected to adapt and cope with my situation more smoothly than most adults are able.

Along with flipping my lifestyle on its back, death's close proximity put my life in a unique perspective that's hard to grasp by someone who hasn't experienced tragedy of a similar magnitude. Without admitting that I don't care about a lot of things anymore, I will say I'm more forgiving and patient than I ever was. The tragedy of Mark's death was a wake-up call for me to never, ever take anything for granted and cherish every second with every person in my life. Like I learned in the worst way possible, life isn't fair and sometimes people's lives end sooner than they should. That's just the way it goes. The best we can do is trust God and use that pain to develop and mature ourselves into better adults.

That's the greatest opportunity I took from my Jet Ski accident: the opportunity to show God's grace through my story of surviving an unlikely situation. In hindsight, I see how He positioned and grew my faith in a foundation that swelled up and eventually sailed me through the roughest waters anyone could imagine. I grew up and was involved in church since I was a child, but nothing could prepare me for this. The most important thing that has come out of these trials, though, is the impact and grace of God in my life. It's hard to say those words without sounding like a cliché, but there's no other way to put it. My story and the pain of my family is an opportunity for witness and testimony for everyone.

For that I'm grateful and for that, I wouldn't change anything.

Wednesday, October 12 (1 ¹/² months after injury)
– An entry from Dad's CaringBridge journal.

We don't know what God's plans are for Kristin and we aren't empowered to make changes, even if we did know. Kristin was given to us by God and has most certainly been a gift. I'm thankful for every minute with her, regardless of her current condition. What I do know is that whatever the outcome, we are here but a short time. Eventually, we will all be healed of whatever ails us – made complete. Our prayers, ALL of our prayers, from this point forward are to focus on Kristin's ability to make the best of what His will gives her and to give us the wisdom to make the right decisions regarding her care. A prayer to make opportunities available to us that will heal her wounds, to be given definitive signs that we are making the right decisions, to never give up the hope of walking again, and to give her the steadfast faith that her life will be made whole.

I loved her when she was born, when she ran to me scared of her first bumblebee, when she fell down and scraped her knee, when she sang her first song in front of our family, when I tickled her and she laughed uncontrollably. I loved her when she broke her arm...the same arm, 3 times, when she slept at night looking like an angel, when she woke up in the middle of the night from a bad dream, when she came home crying because someone had been mean to her, when she came home happy because she made a new friend. I loved her when her room was a mess and I loved her when she proudly proclaimed that she cleaned it and it still looked like a train wreck. I loved her when she hid her report card, when she failed a test, when she didn't make "the cut" for a team, when we looked at each other from across the dinner table and made faces at her sister and mom. I loved her when she told me a secret with a "pinky swear," when I tried to "fix" her hair and she said, "Thanks, Daddy" and went to re-fix it, when she told me "You're my hero." I loved her when she fought with her sister over her clothes being borrowed, when her outfits for school looked like she was dressed to clean the garage, when she told me her sister is her best friend. I loved her when she fought with her mom, when I would find them hugging just seconds later, when she would tell me not to step on the ant because "the ant has a family too." I loved her when I'd find her curled up with our dog, Cody, on her bed, when she wouldn't let me leave without running to tell me goodbye with a hug and a kiss. I loved her when she would still hold my hand whenever I wanted. Kristin, you have made my life complete in so many ways. We're going to get through this. I love you.

Daddy

CHAPTER 2

Children's Hospital Inpatient

N o rest for the weary. Therapy starts at 8:00 am. Ideally, Kristin would be able to sleep until 10:00 then start her sessions, but I suspect they're trying to establish a routine for her by starting so early. Rhonda says she eats very little of her breakfast. When I asked her about it, she proclaimed that the food "tastes like barf." That's my girl! Gotta love that brute honesty.

Kristin's regiment seems to be that she is very sad in the morning. We discussed it being like the movie Groundhog Day. Because of some leftover memory issues from her brain injury, she can't re-live the fun of her visitors. The one thing she does remember id that she has a full day of therapy ahead of her. We can all agree that this can be distressing. Even my stupid jokes along the way don't help.

"Good morning," I blurted to Mom as soon as I opened my eyes. She was on her way across the room to help me put on my pants.

Living in a hospital turned me into an exceptionally light sleeper; the sound of my mother's flat feet walking to the bathroom served as my wake-up call every morning.

"Good morning," she smiled. "Breakfast will be delivered soon. Eat fast before your therapist comes."

I blinked acknowledgement and pushed the incline button on my bedrail. The freedom of sitting at least partially upright without wearing my tortoise-shell back brace was enough for me to sit up as often as possible. I was allowed to be without it as long as my body sat at no straighter than a 45 degree angle so that my spine could heal correctly after surgery. The brace is made of two, hard plastic sheets customized to swallow my entire torso, and held tightly together with beige Velcro straps. Not surprisingly, it's extremely uncomfortable and required for my whole time as an inpatient at Children's Hospital. This was not the sexiest time in my life.

"Okay," I said with little enthusiasm. It was fake, but it was there. "I don't remember what I ordered so it'll be a surprise."

One second after I finished my sentence, two small fists banged on the door. Mom slid across the room and cracked it open. The small hands gave her a beige plate on a beige tray, most likely covering beige food.

"What's it going to be?" I asked Mom, now with forced curiosity.

My short term memory loss makes my life more fun because I forget about things and am genuinely surprised when they resurface later. I uncovered the beige plate and thanked myself for ordering eggs.

"Oh great," I said to the room. "They included a yogurt for my mom."

She grabbed the yogurt cup off my tray and carried it across the room to mix with her granola mixture from home. I surprised myself and ate the tasteless hospital eggs quickly. I only had a few seconds to look around the room before Mom stood up and resumed her trip over to me, sweatpants in hand.

"I'll help you put these on," she said. I was thrilled. It's like she could read my mind.

Before she could reach my bed, another banging on the door. Loud banging was followed by the door swinging open. Tammy, my occupational therapist, pounced into my room like a sick tiger and immediately started fuming at Mom – literally no hesitation.

"Are you putting her pants on?" she asked with an accusing expression and tone. "Put those down. She needs to do that herself. Let her do it."

Now like an enemy, Tammy snatched my sweatpants from Mom's innocent hands and threw them at me like confetti. This is not a party.

I took the pants from where they landed on my bedrail and began the too-long process of pulling them up my too-long legs. I slid first my right leg, then my left into each leg hole and pulled the waistband underneath my butt cheeks. The only way to pass over my butt, I found, is to lay flat on the bed and thrash my body to either side to unweight. I would like to say it's because I have a large, beautiful butt like Beyoncé, but the real reason is I was just weak. If putting on pants is this difficult laying down, I never want to do it sitting up.

"Good job," Tammy said after standing by and watching me struggle in my bed for 5 minutes. I couldn't tell if she was sarcastic or serious, so I gave her a neutral fake smile. "Let me help with these."

She bent down to pick up a pair of T.E.D. hose from the floor. They were tight, spandex-like leggings that the doctor had me put on every morning before getting in my wheelchair. The hospital bed elevated my legs to promote my blood's circulation while I slept, but sitting in my wheelchair is a different story for blood circulation. My brain injury resulted in loss of some connection to my lower body, putting me in danger of blood clots and a guarantee of swollen ankles. I wore the hose as prevention.

More notably, though, T.E.D. hose are tight stockings that clung to my already-shrunken calf muscles and came in a pasty, white color. Everything about those hose made me look like even more of a skinny white girl than I already do. Again, not my sexiest time.

"Give me your foot," Tammy demanded. I picked up my leg at my calf muscle and handed it to her.

At this point my leg muscles had diminished enough to resemble a box of pasta noodles, and it took my conscious thought to take special care of them. One of my first memories in inpatient therapy is Tammy pulling her face too close to mine and spitting "just because you don't feel them doesn't mean they're not there, Kristin." Again and again she would say it. Every time she would spit.

Still, lower body mindfulness took a while to be second nature.

"Okay," Tammy finished. "Let's brush your teeth then I'll walk you to Speech Therapy."

I transferred into my wheelchair and followed her to the bathroom. It was still kind of a big deal for me to be brushing my own teeth; one month ago I didn't have the strength or balance to sit in my wheelchair, much less hold a toothbrush to my mouth. Finally after two never-ending months of hard work, I was able to transfer into my black and orange loaner wheelchair; push myself to the bathroom; and clean all my teeth and whole face. That's called progress.

I didn't even have time to open my mouth to the mirror and admire my clean mouth and face before Tammy grabbed the handlebars of my wheelchair and forced me out of the small bathroom and through our hospital room's door, like it or not.

"Bye Mom," I called behind to me.

She said something in response but I couldn't hear her over the grumpy look Tammy was shooting the world. I don't know what I did to agitate her so much.

She let go of my handles when we rolled past the nurse's station and turned her head to look at me expectantly. Maybe one day pushing my wheelchair won't be so bad, but at that moment it seemed like the worst thing. To avoid the wrath of Tammy, though, I grabbed my push rims and pushed myself the rest of the way to the therapy room. Slowly, but I got there.

"Bye," Tammy snarled as soon as we got within 5 feet of the gym. "Tomorrow we'll work on speed."

Her mouth made a weak smile as she stepped backwards away from me. She said "we'll work on it" as if she was even remotely struggling alongside me. It was dispiriting.

"Bye," I needlessly responded.

Speech Therapy was fine because we played games the whole time. Before my memory came back I struggled with things like association, auditory processing, mouth-muscle weakness, and similar problems that translate into labeling objects in a cartoon and playing Connect Four with my therapist. In that time, my traumatic brain injury was still in control of my body and those exercises were extremely difficult.

By the time my memory loss started to fade and my mind was functioning closer to a normal person, Speech Therapy was less of a necessity and more of a break in my therapy schedule to play games and be successful at activities. It was actually something I looked forward to, and that's saying something. Going to Speech Therapy was my calm before the storm that was my least favorite time of the day: Physical Therapy.

"Great job today," Lisa, my speech therapist, told me. She walked toward the door and opened it with a forced grin on her face. I had humbled her with three consecutive wins at Guess Who and I think she was bitter.

"Thank you," I cheered as I rolled toward the opening. I felt happy and superior.

Immediately when I rolled out of the Speech Therapy room and looked around to the Physical Therapy gym, though, all of my joy vanished. Ahead of me were free weights, padded tables, weighted balls, black exercise mats lined on the floors, and other familiar tools used in my torture.

In addition to the room's visual misery, the instantaneity of my transition from Speech to Physical Therapy gave me no time to mentally callous myself to the fabricated and compulsory enthusiasm that was inevitable with these physical therapists. It seems like they know that no one likes PT so they try to cover it up with happiness and fake laughter. In reality, though, that just makes it worse.

"Hi Kristin," Shaina, my therapist, ran up and shouted at me unnecessarily. "It's really great to see you today." I nodded my head and she continued. "Today we're going to go outside and do some off-roading on the grass. The weather is great."

That explained her overwhelming greeting: she knows how miserable off-roading still is for me, so she was covering it up with exhausting intensity. Again, makes it worse.

"Okay," I responded in a voice of sadness and defeat.

It doesn't matter if I agreed or screamed obscenities at her because she didn't hear me. I watched the back of Shaina's head bounce around the gym to grab her jacket and my wheelchair gloves. She was putting on a good performance.

Shaina led me down the safe hallways of the hospital, through the courtyard, and onto a patch of deadly and unforgiving grass. The expression on my face felt like something Tammy, my occupational therapist, would show on hers, but I didn't care. I hoped everyone would see me and recognize the torture I was being subjected to.

"All right," Shaina said, still maintaining an overly-happy voice. "I want you to start here and push to there." Her fingers pointed at two different and distant points in the grass: the beginning and the end.

I let out a soft "uhhh," and rolled over what was my last seconds on concrete flooring and onto the first patch her finger directed me to. My tires bumped off the hard surface and into the grass aquarium of doom. After a dramatic sigh, I pushed my tires' rims to move my chair forward. I literally did not move.

"I didn't get a good grip," I justified under my breath.

One more attempt and I found this was not the case. The months I spent lying on the hospital bed fighting for my life is also the time my muscles had almost completely disappeared; 3 months in a hospital bed is all it took to erase almost 15 years of activity. That being the case, off-roading on the grass was the hardest thing I'd done in three months and quite possibly my entire life. It was all very dramatic.

"I'll give you a push for momentum," I heard Shaina's voice from behind me.

I felt her grab my wheelchair's handlebars and push me forward effortlessly. Traction from the grass allowed me to float one half inch before I stopped. I gripped my tires' push rims and tried to use the momentum to push farther, but nothing.

Ten minutes and 100 attempts and I was finally and steadily migrating across the grass. I was moving agonizingly slow and my palms were angry red, but I eventually reached my end.

"Okay," I breathed, only barely still sitting up. I hung my arms at my sides for as little effort as possible. "Done."

"We'll work on that more next week," Shaina said with a genuine but malicious smile.

I think she thought she was good. If I had a flip flop in my hand I would chuck it at her head, but I didn't have anything to throw, so I turned to push my chair back onto the sidewalk.

"That's a great idea," I said back to her.

My voice tried to not sound sarcastic, but I don't know how successful that was. Honestly, I wanted to sound sincere – I wanted Shaina to like me.

"I look forward to it," I forced.

The goal of Physical Therapy in the hospital is to learn how to live life in a wheelchair, and I had a hard time accepting that; my determination to rehabilitate myself away from my wheelchair fogged my motivation to accommodate my wheelchair. For that reason, I was impatient with the monotonous exercises of Hospital PT. I was expected to work hard at things I didn't care about and I was convinced they were a waste of time. At that time, I was convinced that steering a wheelchair through a patch of grass was a waste of time. Obviously, I was wrong. In the middle of my torture it was easy to find flaws in my sessions and, better yet, my therapists. I'm sure they were all wonderful people, but I couldn't see that. I was blinded by both discontent with my physical situation and frustration with having to relearn my whole lifestyle.

Like would soon become normal, everyone was watching and I had to put on a show.

My hands were stinging from my outdoor adventure and it was difficult to do anything except roll slowly to my next therapy at the end of the hall. Next on my schedule was the only therapy I enjoyed: Recreational Therapy. I think it's safe to say that I looked forward to it.

Similar to Speech Therapy, Rec. Therapy was most beneficial to me in the times before my memory came back. We would play board games to improve skills that my traumatic brain injury took away: manual dexterity, cognitive ability, logical thought processing, etc. By the time I started remembering, though, it was just an hour at the end of the day to play games. Poker, in my case.

After P.T., we went in for our daily game of Texas Hold 'Em. Kristin really enjoys that game for some reason. There were six players: 2 patents, 3 therapists, and me. Kristin did very well! I was proud! We ended up going head to head a couple of times. Of course, her idea was for us to team us and bring everyone else down, so she was trying to come up with a "secret language" for us to use against everyone else. Her plan was foiled when everyone else folded and we were up against each other. We only had 20 minutes to play today, but we had a good time. She is so funny.

When an hour in Rec. Therapy wasn't enough play time, I had to improvise. As an inpatient in the hospital, you have to make your own fun.

The highlight of yesterday started around 6p.m. Kristin's room was empty when I arrived, but I could hear what sounded like a frat party going on down the hall. As I walked toward the nurse's station, I could see a lot of familiar faces gathered around a table. There was a lot of laughter coming from that table. Kristin had started a Texas Hold 'Em poker game with about 8 of the nurses and staff playing, and another 8 people standing behind them. The game was in full swing! Honestly, I'm surprised the nurses let us keep up the noise level. But they were the ones making the noise! Whenever I saw a nurse walking past the area, they were smiling at the fun that was going on.

The game finally broke around 8:30. Kristin took a break and came back to the game, but I could tell she was worn out. She began to get nauseous, so we called it quits and I had to go back home for the night. Rhonda came back to the hospital for the night. Once again, Kristin took her energy right to the limit!

After the laughter fizzled out and my nausea was starting to take hold, I rolled back to my hospital room and saw Mom sitting in the corner chair with her cell phone pressed to her ear and an open laptop on her lap.

"I did some research on it," she said to the person on the other end of the phone. "I found a place in California we should look into. I'll see what I can find out." She turned around to face me and continued. "Kristin is here. Do you want to talk to her?"

She turned to look at me and smiled the biggest, most welcoming smile. Something was making her excited. This wasn't the first time I walked in on her talking about "places we should try" and "places to look into." I didn't fully understand what she was talking about until later, though. It was like there was something going on right under my nose but I was so wrapped up in my acute therapy that I didn't bother to know about it until later.

I reached out my hand to take the phone and hoped I would hear Dad on the other end. He had literally just left the hospital, but I missed him already.

"Dad?" I said.

"Hey sweetie," I heard his familiar voice. After a day of exhausting hospital living, he is my calming force. "How are you feeling? Still nauseous?"

"I'm okay," I said. "I'm worn out. I'll probably go to bed soon."

We talked for another few minutes before saying goodbye for the night. My days in the hospital didn't give me much to talk about with him and his days in the mortgage business didn't give him much to talk about with me, so conversations didn't last very long. On the days he didn't have a lot of time to stay with us in the hospital, though, those few minutes were my highlight. We made wonderful, but very small, talk for another 5 minutes before saying "goodnight."

"Hi sweetie," Mom's voice sang in my ear after I hung up the phone. "How was Shaina today?"

"The same," I said as I made my way across the room to my bed.

My muscles were fatigued and Mom realized it with my failed attempts to transfer out of my chair.

"Let me help," she chimed.

I heard her familiar flat-footed walking as she came across the room to lift my limp body onto the mattress. I let out a gust of air as my head sunk into the pillow and body relaxed into the sheets. There really is no place in the whole hospital building I would rather be than my bed.

"Here's the remote in case you want it," Mom said. She handed me a beige plastic box attached to my bed rail by a thick, rubber tube.

I mumbled out a "thank you" and pushed the remote button until I saw SpongeBob SquarePants. It was an episode I've seen 100 times, but makes me laugh every time. As an inpatient in the hospital, things that are funny become hilarious; excitement turns to hysteria; and every link to the outside world is treasured. I laid in bed and enjoyed that episode of SpongeBob like it was the first time I had ever watched television.

Mom joined me around 7:30, so I switched off Nickelodeon to find a program we both enjoyed. From there, we watched a marathon of numbing television right into 9:00. I saw her eyes dozing from the corner of my eye, so it was no surprise when she finally spoke up.

"Okay," Mom said in a voice that sounded like she was talking into a pillow. "Let's go to bed. You have a big day of therapy tomorrow and I'm tired."

"Okay Mom," I said with a small laugh in my voice.

I don't know why she was tired – she did almost literally nothing strenuous all day. She walked to my bed to give me a kiss on the forehead before burrowing back into her cot next to me.

"Goodnight," Mom's small voice came from the corner of the room.

"Goodnight Mama," I said at full volume.

I lay on my side in my stiff hospital bed for what seemed like the next hour listening to phone calls, beeps, and the buzzing from the nurse's station outside our door. Like New York City, Children's Hospital never sleeps.

Today, Kristin exemplified the will of a warrior; her drive was more powerful that it has ever been. All of her therapists raved about her efforts. She even told her Education Therapist that she wants to be smarter than she used to be. She's going to be smarter, faster, stronger than before.

Here's the compassion of a saint. Tonight before I left, she told me "I'm actually glad this happened to me instead of one of my friends. I don't think I would be able to handle it if this happened to one of my friends. It would be too hard." Sometimes, I can't comprehend the size of Kristin's heart. It is capable of exuding the deepest love that a person can have for others. She lies cripples for what may be the rest of her life, but can only think of others. There is no anger or resentment, only compassion. What can we learn from this?

I've always told my children that no one can make you feel any way; you control your own feelings. This has always been good when they would fuss at each other and say "she made me feel bad," etc. I think I've found an exception to my own rule. Kristin has made me feel like the best father and person in the world. It was always right there in front of me, but I didn't take the time to realize it. I am fortunate to have a special person like her and, because she is forced to be around me right now, I'm getting to know her better. Sadly, it took an accident of this magnitude to make me spend more time with her. If you're a father and have a daughter, don't make the same mistake I did. Your relationship with your daughter(s) is unique and can easily be wasted by being too busy. Take the time to make her your best friend. Your life will be enriched beyond belief and your heart will love deeper than ever before. My tears of pain have been replaced by tears of joy. This feeling has been indelibly etched.

CHAPTER 3

Reverse Trick or Treating

"What time are Katie and Katy coming?" I nearly shouted to Mom when I saw her body roll over to turn off our 7:30am alarm clock.

"They're coming after they get out of school," she responded in a sleepy voice. "After you get out of PT."

"Cool," I said with a pervasive and eager smile. "Maybe my therapies won't be so bad today because it's Halloween." Mom turned her head to me and we gave each other a long and meaningful look. She snapped out of it first.

"Tammy will be here soon," I heard her say and climb out of her cot beside me. "You should get dressed and sit up in your chair."

Every other morning the process of getting from lying in bed to sitting up in my wheelchair is a long, procrastinated one. This morning, however, I have something to look forward to. I am looking forward to Physical Therapy, otherwise my most hated and dreaded therapy, because it's the last thing that stands in the way of myself and my two best friends coming to the hospital for a Halloween celebration.

"Good morning," Tammy flung open our door and sang. Her face is usually in a frown and voice usually monotone, so I was a little bit surprised. "Happy Halloween."

She tossed me a piece of taffy candy and grabbed my sweatpants off the chair beside my bed.

"Thank you," I said with genuine appreciation and still some surprise. Like a catcher in a baseball game I caught the taffy, dropped it at my side, and brought my open hands back in front of my chest. I was anticipating catching my sweatpants that Tammy aggressively throws at me every morning.

"After you get dressed and brush your teeth I'll walk you to Speech Therapy." She spoke with an inflection in her voice that was so sweet sounding and so unexpected from her lips. It almost made me uncomfortable.

I let down my pant-catching hands and started to push my legs off the side of the bed to transfer into my wheelchair. Like she was waiting for my vulnerability, Tammy chucked my pants at me from across the room, landing on my head to drape over my eyes.

"Why didn't you catch them?" she asked with genuine-sounding confusion.

I couldn't tell if she was being serious or playing with me, so I responded with a universal fake laugh and "yeah." My body was still weak, reflexes still slow, and mind still recovering from a traumatic brain injury. Making great friends with my occupational therapist is not and could not be at the top of my priorities. I'm sure this wasn't her heart break.

After I was dressed and teeth cleaned, Tammy walked me to meet Lisa, my speech therapist. Lisa & I ran through a routine of word associations, picture associations, memory recall, and the rest of the hours' worth of semantic memory exercises intended to bring my mind back to what it was before my accident. At this point, it was kind of fun.

The Speech Therapy room dumped me into the Physical Therapy gym. My Occupational and Speech Therapies are usually somewhat of a breeze, but Physical Therapy is a whole different ball game. It is the salt on the wound that is an inpatient hospital status.

Actually, it's more like a pound of salt dumped onto an amputation.

I endured the routine of rolling over obstacles, making uneven transfers, and doing bicep curls until my hour of torture was finally over. Every exercise I did in Physical Therapy was aimed at making me a more independent wheelchair user. It was beneficial I guess, but also terrible. My heart and my mind were on a whole different planet. There are no wheelchairs on my planet.

I was finally released from Physical Therapy with sore arms and a throbbing upper back. All that discomfort I could barely feel, though, because I was so stoked on my friends coming to see me. I was wrong about my therapists respecting the holiday and going easy on me, but I was right about my therapies being better than usual. My excitement blurred out my misery.

"Hey sweetie," Mom's voice sang when I rolled into our hospital room. I decided to skip Recreational Therapy today so I could get ready for my friends. That was significant seeing as, besides lying my bed, Rec. Therapy is the only consistently pleasing element of the place. By not being there, I was giving someone else a chance to win at Texas Hold 'Em.

Just kidding.

Like most days, Mom was sitting on a chair in the corner of the room with an open book and reading glasses on the tip of her nose. "How was PT?"

I answered her question with an exaggerated expression of dread.

"The same," I said and lowered the side handlebar of my hospital bed. "I'm going to lie down until Katie and Katy get here."

With three wobbly, tired movements I transferred onto the side of the bed and fell back onto my arms with my legs hanging off the side. From the corner of the room, Mom saw my struggle and stood up from her chair.

"I'll help you," she said. I fell back and she grabbed my ankles to hover my legs until they aligned with my limp body. "They're not coming until after dinner so you can rest for a while."

Before she even finished her sentence my eyes were closed and I was drifting to sleep. The three months that I laid idle in a hospital bed almost literally drained me of all my endurance, and a morning full of mindless therapy was enough to turn me into the smallest baby. In one perspective it's a good thing because I could sleep away the brain-numbing atmosphere of an inpatient hospital ward, but it's also a bad thing because sleep feels like a waste of time. Either way you look at it, though, I slept.

Two hours later, I woke to the sound of a knock on my door. One knock was followed by the opening door knob, followed by a quiet scream from Katy.

"Hi," Katie said enthusiastically when she walked through the threshold and into my room.

"Hey guys," I responded. I was trying to act cool, where in my mind I was drooling with excitement. "I'm almost ready."

I transferred out of my bed with surprising ease and rolled across the room to the bathroom. From where I sat under the sink, I heard Mom giving Katie and Katy instructions for our hospital operation.

"I put the candy in this bag," she said. "Ask the nurses which rooms you're allowed to go into then give each kid 2 or 3 pieces." A silence followed Mom's words and I imagined Katy and Katie nodding their heads and taking the bag.

I rolled out of the bathroom into the cramped hospital room where the 3 of them stood. On her head, Katy had a headband with two unrecognizable shapes coming from behind each ear. Katie was wearing a pair of oversized, purple glasses that reminded me of the large eye glasses I wore from 3rd grade until middle school, nicknamed the "glasses that gave me rashes." They were appropriately dressed for the Halloween occasion and the only costume I had was my frail inpatient hospital face.

"Most of the people in the rooms won't know you're there," Mom continued. "You can just say 'Happy Halloween' and leave a piece of candy on their bedside table. They can't eat it because they have feeding tubes, but maybe their nurses will enjoy it."

We nodded our heads, put together the last of our costumes, and filed out of the room to the nurse's station.

"Do you guys want to go into the long term care unit first?" a nurse met us in the hallway and asked. I guess someone tipped her off on what we were doing. Either that, or our lame costumes gave us away. "I'll walk with you and show you which rooms you can go into. Some of the kids can't have visitors."

"Okay," I hesitated. "Sure."

Katie, Katy, and I looked at each other with wide eyes. The long term care unit was unfamiliar territory – it is kept shut and separate from the rest of the patients with two thick, black doors. Behind those doors is a ward of kids that are sick enough to live as an inpatient in the hospital until they turn 18, their insurance stops making payments, and they have to find an adult facility to relocate to.

"Good," the nurse said. "Follow me."

She pushed open the heavy doors and led us into a hallway that looked identical to my own. The three of us walked through the hall with a bag full of fun size candy and our Halloween costumes, greatly varying in intensity. We handed out our candy to a new group of 20-

25 sick children, and only made about half of them smile. Those kids differed from the kids in the acute care unit because they have chronic conditions that don't take as much of a physical toll on their bodies; some of the kids looked deceivingly healthy. Some stared at us blankly and took a piece of candy, some thanked us with a whisper, but most lay on their beds like vegetables.

Each hospital room was a new experience with only one constant: the smell. There was a stale, sour aroma that followed everyone and everything in the building, and going in and out of patient's rooms made me extra aware of it. In my opinion, Mom and I were the only things that smelled normal, but that's probably because we smelled like the hospital, too. Everyone likes their own brand.

Nearing the end of our hospital tour, we followed the nurse into the last rooms in the long term care hallway.

"Hi Kristin," I heard someone say from behind me. The voice was familiar. I looked to my left and was thrilled to see it belonged to Rashad, a friend I made at the poker table in Recreational Therapy. He was a quadriplegic boy, about the same age as me, who was hit by a stray bullet from some kind of drug gang in downtown Richmond. He had no one to take care of him at home, so he was living at Children's Hospital until he turned 18. Rashad was my buddy.

"Hey Rashad," I said, feeling cool because I had an inpatient friend. "We're reverse trick or treating."

I rolled to him and offered my open bag. Without hesitation he reached his hand into the opening and grabbed a Snickers, two Kit Kat bars, and a Butterfinger. He took more than the other children, but I didn't say anything because we were friends.

We sat and smiled at each other for another 30 seconds after he picked his prize.

"Okay Rashad," I said. "We have more rooms to visit before it gets too late. I'll see you at Rec. Therapy tomorrow."

That wasn't a lie because we really did have a few more rooms to visit, but I mostly said it to avoid an inevitable block in conversation.

Rashad and I had almost literally nothing in common aside from both living at the hospital and wanting a friend.

"Bye," he responded. His voice didn't sound as affectionate as I would have hoped, but I smiled big so Katie and Katy would be impressed.

We left Rashad and gave candy to 2 more kids before we had reverse trick-or-treated every room in the long term and acute care units of Children's Hospital. I tried to drag it out by rolling slowly to prolong the time with my friends for as long as possible, but we were finally done.

"Did you guys have fun?" Mom asked when we returned to my hospital room.

"Yes we did," I said with enthusiasm that was still lingering. "We gave candy to a lot of kids and couldn't go into a lot of rooms. We saw Rashad, though."

"Oh you guys met Kristin's friend Rashad," she said with a raised voice.

"Yeah we did," Katie said. "We met Rashad." The inflection in her voice made me hope she would tell an anecdote or say something else about it, but she stopped talking.

"Okay," Katy looked at the clock and said. "We should leave because I have homework and we have school in the morning. We'll come back to visit soon."

"Okay," I said. I knew they had to leave eventually, but it still surprised me. More, I was disappointed.

All three of us were in our sophomore year of high school and I missed it more than anything my accident took from me. I missed living like a normal teenager. I missed the structure of going to high school early in the morning, being surrounded by my friends for 6 uninterrupted hours, learning new things, and having my only and greatest responsibility the schoolwork I am assigned. I missed when my greatest concern was how I looked to an attractive boy at lunchtime, and to ignore all of those worries while I run around during field hockey or lacrosse practice afterwards. Going to school and being active are things young people take for granted, but they're the things I craved more than anything else.

"Bye guys," I said, trying again to make my voice casual. Katie reached down to give me a hug and Katy stuck out her fist to pound.

I watched the back of their heads as they walked away, and felt so much sadness and so much jealousy. I was jealous of their ability to walk and jealous of their ability to leave. Having visitors was the best part of my time in the hospital because it showed me people didn't forget about me completely, but it's also the worst part because they leave and return to the outside world I so badly wanted to occupy.

My freshman year at Deep Run High School was the best year of my life. I was a competition cheerleader, member of the school field hockey team, and captain of the lacrosse team. My constant participation in sports meant my body was healthy, my social life was refined, and my self-confidence was through the roof. I was able to maintain an even tan on my skin, a tight body, and a cute butt. Sophomore year was supposed to be a continuation of those things, but my accident ruined that for me. The longer I spent in the hospital and as I continued to understand my inability, the deeper that sunk in. My life would never be the same. Actually, not even close. I was broken.

"Let's get ready for a bath," Mom said from behind me. I was thankful for a distraction from the tears that were so close to falling from my eyes. "The nurse is coming to wash you soon."

"Okay," I said, snapping back into my inpatient reality. "I'll get my clothes ready."

Just as I spoke, Janice, a night nurse, opened the door and rolled a nylon "bed" into my room. Because I still couldn't sit upright without my turtle-shell back brace, my body and hair had to be washed by a nurse while I lay horizontally on a waterproof table. Having my head massaged and body scrubbed wasn't the worst thing about hospital life, but it certainly wasn't the best thing. Actually, it was humiliating.

"You've had a big day," Janice remarked. We continued to small talk while she washed me. A conversation took my mind off of my disdain, at the very least. It is a little bit uncomfortable to be too friendly with someone who washes my creases, but even worse is silence.

"Okay," Janice said loudly and turned off the water. Her voice echoed in the small, tile bathroom. "You look tired." I nodded my head and looked at her with a straight mouth. "Here's your night gown to put on."

She grabbed and chucked my gown at me then spun around to give me privacy, I guess. I don't know why she bothered with that, though – two minutes ago she was washing under my armpits and butt cheeks – it was a little too late for privacy.

After a couple of minutes Janice turned around, saw that I was dressed, and grabbed the handles of my bed to wheel me back to my hospital room. We did not speak.

"Hey," Mom said when Janice opened the door and rolled the long shower bed inside.

She was standing next to my bed with the hair dryer and a buttered toothbrush in her hands, silently offering to let me stay in bed instead of returning to my wheelchair to get ready. My body and mind were exhausted from a full day of therapy, friends, trick or treating, and leftover candy. I brushed my teeth in bed and spit into a plastic cup that Mom emptied in the sink. She brushed and dried the final tangles in my hair as I peacefully dozed to sleep. We had a good system.

Friends and family are the one of the only things that got me through my time in the hospital. Thanks to the Lord, I was unconscious for the initial and most brutal periods after my accident. My traumatic brain injury caused short term memory loss and my inability to remember my first weeks of consciousness. Halloween with my friends was one of my first and best memories of being an inpatient at Children's Hospital.

Saturday, December 17 (4 months after injury)
– An entry from Dad's CaringBridge journal.

Today was Kristin's Homecoming celebration. For those of you that came out, you felt the emotion, I'm sure. For those of you that missed it, it was incredible. We believe there was at least 400 people in our front yard and lined on the streets. We took Kristin to lunch at her favorite place, the Pita Pit. I started out when we left by telling her she looked pretty enough to be on television. We ate lunch and went to Walgreens. While we sat in the car, I asked "Have you ever thought about what you would say if you could speak to all the people who have helped and supported you along the way?" She said "No, I don't really know how I would thank so many people." I told her "You never know – you may one day get the chance to do it. You better be prepared!" So, she stuck up her thumb and proceeded to talk into a make-believe microphone for me.

We drove home and into our street and began to see a lot of parked cars. I said to her, "It looks like someone is having a party!" Then we drove through the sea of people on the side of the road leading to our house. It was the most amazing sight – people holding signs, jumping up and down, all smiling at Kristin in the front seat of the car. Kristin's jaw was dropped the entire time. She said "This is all for me?" I said, "Welcome home, Kristin."

Channel 6 was there and interviewed her. The Richmond Times Dispatch was there, along with a lot of incredible people who have supported her over the past 3.5 months since her accident. Kristin and our family were so, incredibly moved.

I have to say that through this I've learned a deeper meaning of love. I've learned that there is no end to what can be accomplished. I've learned that the love of a daughter continually grows stronger every day, that the love of a sister cannot be duplicated. I've learned that the love of a mother is tireless, and the love of a best friend knows absolutely no boundaries. Most of all, I've learned that the love of a community is irreplaceable in our little corner of the world. We could not move from here and experience the same emotion and support as what you have all given us. You have made my little girl so, very happy. God bless each and every one of you.

CHAPTER 4

Project Walk

Remember the research my parents were doing when I was inpatient at Children's Hospital? About two weeks before my discharge in December, I finally found out what it was about.

While I was in therapy learning how to do simple things like put on my pants and transfer into a bed, my parents were searching online for not only a gym for me to go to because I was in a wheelchair, but somewhere for me to go to get out of a wheelchair.

I have been praying that I will make the right decision regarding the path we take in Kristin's healing. One day after I prayed that prayer, things happened that were so obvious on a decision to be made. This type of "sign" hasn't happened so crystal clear to me in my lifetime until then. It's a bit much to write but, in summary, I was redirected to pursue a treatment center in Carlsbad, California called Project Walk. After checking it out, it's a legitimate chance for Kristin to improve with dramatic success. No gimmicks, no tricks, but rather hard work and definitive success.

We've decided that Rhonda and Kristin will go for 5 weeks in January. If this works out, we may end up going back this summer. It is fairly disruptive to us due to the distance but, again, I've received some very definitive messages that this is the route to take. I thank God for His way of showing us where to turn.

With an acute injury like mine, every minute counts; the fresher the injury is, the easier it is to take back what was lost in the injury. Our bodies are like math equations, chemistry formulas, or any other terrible skill we were expected to master in school: the information is fresh and accessible right after we learn it but, as time goes on and the information is not accessed, it becomes less clear until finally it's unattainable. The same goes with our bodies after a traumatic accident; the combination of trauma and scar tissue causes our bodies forget how to carry out movements or sensations below injury level and, over time, they lose the ability to compensate for the lost connections.

With that knowledge in their heads, my parents lit a flame under their butts. Two weeks after I was discharged from the hospital I was on the plane to Carlsbad, California to start on the first of many long, bumpy roads toward rehabilitation. I hardly had a chance to enjoy life back at home before I was leaving again. I was going to California for five weeks, though, so this is definitely not a complaint.

It was further shown to me that the right decision is to have Kristin go through extensive intense physical rehabilitation before considering invasive surgery. I was told by more than one person that we are in the very early stages and that her youth has much to tell/show us. The key here is that we are being

*very proactive in her healing process. Kristin has been explained everything
we're doing and she has been equally as proactive. She stands ready to do
whatever it takes, including intense physical exercise. She is in combat mode and
ready to take on all obstacles. God bless her and her huge heart.*

"Sit by that machine and I'll be there in a minute," Travis called at
me from the back of the gym within two seconds of arriving.

He pointed across the room to a strange looking piece of equipment.
The gym was filled with machines and contraptions I had never seen
before, but I was excited to try them all. The world of disability was
still exciting and full of unfamiliarity. Because I was still fresh out of the
hospital, I was excited to take it all in.

I spun around and saw him grabbing the ankles of a familiar-looking
girl for a transfer. I recognized the girl's face not because I had ever
talked to her or knew her name, but because I had been working out
alongside her 4 hours every day for the past month. We had exchanged
smiles and/or a head nod many times, but were always too preoccupied
for dialogue.

This is a similar story with everyone I saw at the gym: familiar faces
then it stops. I will never know all of their stories of disability, but we
were all united in one goal: overcoming it. At $100 an hour, there is no
time for friends.

I rolled my wheelchair backwards until it knocked into a diagonal-
framed machine against the wall. There, I sat for only 2 seconds before
Travis walked over to me. Those were my last seconds of peace.

"All right," Travis said as he speed-walked across the gym toward
me. "We're going to start on the Total Gym then go over to the wall."

His eyes lingered on mine for an extra second. I'm pretty sure he
was waiting for me to groan or throw my head back in protest, but
I refused to give him that satisfaction. Wall exercises are infamously
awful, but I hadn't discovered my dislike yet; I was only three weeks
out of the hospital and 5 months into my spinal cord injury – still in
the honeymoon phase. Between accommodating my new body and

making my world wheelchair accessible, I didn't leave time or effort for aversion. Still, though, the thought of working out with a wall pressing against my spine didn't thrill me.

> *I am still in awe of Kristin's upbeat spirit. She makes me so proud with her determination. Every day, she tells me something new that she has accomplished. At this point, most of her "new" things have to do with new machines or exercises she's doing. The focus right now is her core strength. Imagine not having an abdominal control from about 4 inches above your naval. Imagine if your balance was basically non-existent and every move right or left scares you because there's nothing to catch you except your arms when you hit the next thing coming your way...the ground. Kristin's workouts will progressively build those vital muscles. It takes a fair amount of mental strength, along with physical strength, to keep herself going through these workouts. God bless Kristin. She's trying so hard—you can see it in her face. She wants to walk so bad.*

"That sounds great," I said with forced-but-natural-sounding enthusiasm. Intentionally, my positivity dismissed his conversation. I was in control.

Without saying a word, Travis waved his hand toward my legs and I pushed myself to the edge of my seat cushion for a transfer to the Total Gym. Travis and I coordinated lifting my body and I drifted onto the padded glide board.

For the next 20 minutes he sat on a thin, metal footplate and manipulated my knees and legs. Among other things, he moved them in and out of a squat position, causing my body to slide up and down, over and over. All of his movements were slow so I could follow along in my mind and allow my brain to relearn how to make connections to my lower body.

My paralysis is based on my brain's inability to create new pathways, or bridges, over the scar tissue that formed after my accident, to send commands for lost movement and sensation to my lower body. What does that look like? It looks like red burns on my thighs from carrying a dinner plate I didn't know was hot on the bottom. I have scars from my foot falling off my wheelchair's footplate and my toes scraping the cement, leaving a trail of blood and nothing to warn me except horror in other people's faces. I've had 2 rounds of skin grafts on my butt from a misplaced harness used alongside leg braces and a treadmill during a workout, leaving me with third degree burns and pain I was oblivious to. Paralysis not only took away function in my lower body, it turned into a high maintenance, unwelcome intruder to my whole body.

Those circumstances and that inability is what I'm working so hard to overcome. The more times I tell my brain to access my lower half, the more opportunity it has to send down those signals and cement those pathways. The better shape my body is in, the easier it is for connections to be made and the cement to be poured. That's one reason conversation between me and Travis during my workouts was limited: so I could concentrate on my brain signals and focus all my effort on my workout.

The other reason, though, is we had almost literally nothing in common. The hours I spent at Project Walk were consumed by neglected fake smiles and near silence. Travis is attractive to look at and a fairly good athletic trainer, but that's as far as he went with me.

"Okay," he mumbled at the end of 2 sets of 30 squat-like movements on the Total Gym. "Let's move down to the floor and over to the wall."

Again, he held his eyes on mine for an extra second and I kept my face as neutral as possible. My heart was filling with dread in anticipation of the discomfort of the wall, but I couldn't let that show. I couldn't let him win. He grabbed my ankles from the footplate and, again, we worked together to put my body on the matted floor.

"Now," he said slowly, watching my face closely. "Scoot as close as you can to the wall."

I pushed from my arms to unweight my body and slid across the mat without making eye contact. My eyes were focused on the floor and I hid emotion from my face to protect from Travis seeing any kind of reaction. My efforts at secrecy were likely overlooked and definitely over dramatic but, at the very least, it gave me something to occupy my mind away from the stuffy gym environment and uncomfortable relationship with my trainer.

Under Travis' watchful eyes, I sat flat against the wall and endured 3 sets of 25 touchdowns, high V, T, and low V's with my arms. The posture of sitting so close to the wall forces me into a position of pressure on my lower back, causing my shoulder and abdomen muscles to be in constant contraction, and rerouting all my body's tension to the muscles in my neck. The wall takes away my opportunity to compensate my balance with other body parts, resulting in me swimming around in circles until I fall into alignment with my ever-moving arms. It is all very stressful.

"Good job on that," came Travis' insincere voice at the end of my last set of what seemed like 80 repetitions. "You're getting better. Think about driving your hips into the mat to ground you."

I nodded my head with an annoyed expression on my face. I was annoyed with myself for my struggle and annoyed with him for witnessing it.

"I think we'll go to the gait trainer next," Travis' voice sang from above me.

A long smile spread across my face. Out of all the machines available to my workouts, the gait trainer is my favorite – it is my reward. The machine is made of two detached footplates that move up, down, forward, and backwards to mimic walking. As a participant, I wear a harness to support the weight of my body, each of my feet in a foot cradle for support, and both hands on bars running alongside the machine for core stabilization. A mirror in front allows me to watch myself and correct any imperfections in my standing posture.

For me, the most important part of walking on a gait trainer is the mirror in front. It allows me to see myself standing upright – something I have dreamed of and worked toward since late 2005. Sometimes the picture of an able-bodied Kristin is hard to retrieve in my memory and it's helpful to see myself standing up at very possibility. It reminds me of what I work so hard for, and that's helpful.

"We'll spend the last 45 minutes of your time on there," Travis told me. "When you come back this afternoon I have a bunch of core exercises planned. It's going to be fun."

"Fun" is not the word I would have chosen.

"Okay," I said with a smile. I was still trying to be as pleasant as possible. "That is good."

My tone was not sarcastic but he could probably read between the lines. I dropped myself into my wheelchair and rolled across the gym toward the gait trainer. From there I transferred into the hard, rectangle seat and strapped my knees against two pads.

Travis sank below me and double checked the fastenings on my feet. In my imagination, he was crouching down to hide a face of adoration of my almost unreasonably and consistent positive attitude and good looks. That probably wasn't the case, though – maybe he really did just need to check the fastenings. Again, amusing myself was sometimes the only way to get through those hours.

The thought behind the gait trainer is very similar to the Total Gym: put my body through the same, repetitive movements of walking with hopes that my muscle memory will kick in and legs start carrying out the movements themselves. Alongside core strengthening, this concept is central to rehabilitation after a spinal cord injury.

The other central component of my rehabilitation is who I'm alongside. There's a difference between trainers or therapists who truly care about me, and those who train me because it's their job. Someone who takes the time to know me and my disability on a personal level and accommodates the hiccups and struggles that come with my situation, is worth my time. Someone who does that without flinching or running away like so many of my peers, is one worth keeping.

On the other side, a trainer who only goes through the motions and shows little interest beyond the 1-2 hour workout and their paycheck – that's my deal breaker. Even Travis, as disconnected as we were, cared more than that. That's the reason I kept my mouth shut during those calloused workout sessions. He cared.

I spent the remainder of my morning on the gait trainer machine, letting it move my body in the same way of a person walking with full, knee high steps on a treadmill. There was no dialogue between Travis and I except an occasional demand to "move your hips to the right" or "put more weight in your heels." I was okay with that, though. I was focused, mesmerized by an upright Kristin in the mirror.

"Your time is up, girl," Travis blurted to me, always too soon. Forty five minutes of watching his slithering eyes moving to the clock on the wall – not very sneaky.

"Okay," I breathed. The gait trainer robbed me of any and all remaining energy. "I'm done."

As quickly and safely as I could, I helped Travis free my body from the harness and straps of the gait trainer machine. My entire body was fatigued and my mind was already on break – I just had to let my body catch up.

"I'll see you in a couple hours," he shouted from behind me.

The same second I returned to my wheelchair, I was rolling away from both Travis and the concept of exercise. I had 2 hours of lunch break and I did not intend to spend one more minute than I had to hanging around my trainer whom I could barely tolerate. I waved my hand above my head at Travis' words, and kept rolling.

Mom was sitting in the corner chair of the waiting room with reading glasses on the tip of her nose and her eyes softly shut. Like most days, she had fallen asleep to the images of Southern Living, House Beautiful, or a similar home decorating magazine.

"Mama," I said in a soft but urgent voice. Her eyes slowly opened to look at my face that was inches away from hers. "I'm done working out. Let's go eat lunch."

"Okay," she said in a sleepy voice. "I packed us a lunch to eat by the beach."

I looked down to her open purse and saw two Ziploc bags of sandwiches and two mini water bottles.

"That's good," I whispered to her. My body was so tired that a whisper is all I could manage. "Let's go before I have to come back."

She let out a soft "uhhh" as we picked up our things from the waiting room floor – her purse and my sweater – and left through the glass doors. My body was beyond tired, even exhausted, from the morning workout. It's the same exhaust I remember feeling after an all-day field hockey camp or a 2-hour-long competition cheerleading practice. It's an exhaust I crave, a feeling I will do almost anything to have again. Project Walk could get me there.

"Okay," Mom's soft voice whispered.

She nodded her head peacefully and grabbed her car keys from the table next to her chair. My eyes were sleepy and movements slow, but Mom's turkey sandwiches somehow could replenish my energy for my afternoon workout. That, and a picnic on a California beach.

Project Walk was my first encounter with unconventional rehabilitation after my accident and the beginning of my body's return. While I was still an inpatient in the hospital, my parents were already researching options for me – they refused to accept the doctor's prognosis of my disability or, rather, inability. They turned to the Internet to find not just a facility to work out my paralyzed body, but a facility that believes in and supports our dream of getting me back on my feet. They wanted back the hope that my doctors stole when they said I will never move or feel below my injury level. Project Walk in Carlsbad, California was their answer.

The mindset of the people I met in California is unparalleled to any place I've been able to find on the East Coast and believe me— I've looked. I've exhausted every opportunity that has become available in my home city of Richmond, Virginia: a docile physical therapist volunteering from my church; a trainer who sweat on and around me to my distraction; an impressive looking man who tricked me out of my time and money; multiple trainers who refuse to push me to my limits because they believe trying to walk after a spinal cord injury is a waste of time; and more who didn't make an effort to understand my disability. I did find one good one, though: Sheila. I met her while she was with another client at Project Walk, and she was better than I could have asked for. She was trained by California trainers, lived in the same city as I did, and went to my church. Also she's one of my favorite people to be around. With her attitude and capability, Sheila was an answered prayer in the otherwise closed-minded state of Virginia.

The difference between those California trainers and my East Coast trainers (except for Sheila) is their mindset. With my long journey toward an able body, I was introduced to the power of the mind-body connection. At Project Walk and a few places I've visited since then, I've seen it put into practice. I've learned that the human brain is limitless and nothing about our bodies has to be permanent. I believe I can overcome this disability. I will not allow my paralysis to define me.

Most importantly, Project Walk introduced me to a different kind of workout – one that works out my nervous system instead of just my muscles. The main difference between the two is that muscle-building workouts end or plateau when your body reaches a point where it's too tired to benefit from further repetition. Muscle-building workouts are limited to physical ability.

Workouts of the nervous system, on the other hand, use a lot of imagination and even more repetition. The plan is to push yourself to beyond your limits. It takes a strong body, yes, but an even stronger will to push. Walking on a treadmill, as example, is a nervous system workout and one of my favorites. In my case I have to be strapped in a harness and my legs put into motion by a therapist. Along with my body going through the movements, I concentrate my mind on the sensations and imagery in hopes my brain will eventually remember how to carry out the motion of walking. My brain and my body work concurrently.

I learned about the systematization of movement/sensation and quickly discovered a passion for the human body. After my first of seven visits to California, I had foundation enough to manipulate and problem solve around most issues of a spinal cord injury. My new and more refined understanding of the human body brought me closer to my dream of moving and feeling my whole body at my request.

Again, it's all about repetition. The scar tissue that grew at my site of injury acts as a road block for my brain signals; my brain can't communicate with my body below my injury level. Repetition is good because when I continuously send commands to my lower body, those signals will eventually create that bridge over the tissue and to my lower limbs. When that happens, I will be normal again.

Fresh out of the hospital and at the time of my first visit to California, my injury was classified as "complete," meaning I had zero feeling or movement below injury level. Unlike doctors in Virginia, Project Walk gave me hope that my injury isn't permanent; they told me I can regain what I lost and rehabilitate away from my neurological disorder. They showed me that movement and sensation in my lower body are not as much of an impossibility as the doctors said.

As soon as I returned home from California to the East Coast, I put my new attitude into practice: I decided I want to wiggle my toes. I spent endless hours on my bed, staring at my feet, sending down toe-wiggling-signals. Endless hours. My toes would not move, but I wasn't giving up.

Working out at Project Walk and my persistence after I got home is what gave me my first, most important return: tingles. When my mind is focused on a section of my paralyzed body, I have what feels like the legs of 1,000 little bugs dancing on my skin. Later developed, those bugs move from dancing to racing when something is happening to my body, whether it be pain, a full bladder, hot/cold temperatures, or pressure. I started getting the tingling sensation only after many months of post-California focus, but I knew those tingles were the beginning of something good. Something really good.

Here's the cool part:

The bugs started racing all the way down my legs, to my toes, and I eventually saw movement in the big toe of my left foot. My world, again, flipped absolutely upside down.

"This is why I work so hard," I remember telling my mom. "Something is finally happening."

Almost every night since then I focus on my lower body while I'm falling asleep. My prayers have moved from a somewhat naïve "let me walk again," to a more specific "carry brain signals over the scar tissue to my lower body" or simply "give me a connection." The result of my nightly concentration, hard workouts, and ceaseless prayers is my body's ability to send the racing bugs to squeeze my butt' point my feet; feel pressure and a full bladder sensation; and move my legs sideways. Sending those signals is a meditation for me, almost. It's my form of meditation.

Wiggling toes were my first demonstration of the power of my mind and the importance of a mind-body connection. With my reach toward restoring my body's ability, I practiced and achieved a new level of awareness that allows me to tap into my body's power to rebuild itself. Movement in my big toe was just the beginning of a new and endlessly exciting chapter in my life: The Healing Chapter.

All that excitement led to my recognition that results from my workouts are possible and very much tangible. When I woke up from a coma in the hospital, I had a choice to make: give up or get movin'. The easy way, of course, is to give up and accept what comes. But, in this situation, the easy way wasn't a choice for me. The easy way wasn't good enough.

Return of toe movement and the possibility of recovery is what motivates me. I easily became obsessed with regaining movement and sensation I thought I lost. With my body's awakening, I realized I really only misplaced them.

Wiggling toes were just the beginning.

CHAPTER 5

SCI Step

W e have found a new place for Kristin to go for rehab. She and
Rhonda will leave for Ohio next Sunday where Kristin will
attend SCI Step for one week. She's very excited because it will
involve massage therapy, Electrical Muscle Stimulation (EMS) therapy
and, she says, "It's something new." These types of therapies are different
from Project Walk in some ways, so we're hoping to see another level of
improvement. Kristin wants to walk so badly. We're still very cognizant
that if God wants it to happen, it will be so. But it is so very difficult to be
patient when you're living through this situation.

"Where is this place?" Mom asked as we drove around the desolate streets of Mason, Ohio.

It was nine o' clock in the morning and my first day of working out at SCI Step, a rehabilitation gym in the middle of nowhere. Ohio was the destination spot for Spring Break of my sophomore year of high school. It wasn't a beach or resort like the places kids my age visited on Spring Break, but I'm the last to complain about that. I had returned to school only 3 months earlier after getting home from Project Walk, so my intensity was still at its peak; working out was my new love and pastime.

"I don't know," I said. "It doesn't look like much is going on in this part of town." I looked out the window at the never-ending commercial farm land. "But we're in Mason, Ohio, Mom. I don't think there's much going on anywhere."

My spirits were low and my voice was sunken.

Mom nodded her head and forced a smile of agreement. Our car rolled into a park of warehouse buildings that reminded me of the gym where I used to have cheerleading practice: 5 rows of 8-10 tan, rectangular box buildings lined against each other. They were surrounded with no outside landscaping or décor, and a density hung in the air that brought your breathing to consciousness.

Mom parked our car in front of the rectangle building with a small sign that said "SCI Step." There was a spinal cord emblem next to the letters that was faded and extremely unexciting to me. I tried to smother my disenchantment and have an open mind, but Mason, Ohio was chipping away at the small amount of Spring-Break-enthusiasm I felt on the airplane trip out of Richmond.

When I reached the door of the building, I opened it and saw a meager and vacant reception desk with books and papers scattered on top. Sensing people in the next room, I turned to see the backs of three therapists crowding around a small window in a small room. The room looked about the size of my garage and it had two large tables, a pile of dumbbells, and a stack of mats in the corner.

"Hello Beales," shouted a small, energetic blonde woman who turned and walked toward us. "We've been looking forward to your arrival." She was small just like everything else in the gym.

Mom waved her hand and I put a big, bogus smile on my face. These are the moments fake smiles are made for.

The woman, I later learned was named Michelle, motioned me into the gym and pointed to a short table against the wall.

"Let's get started," she said with a dizzying smile. "We're going to do an evaluation first. I need to learn your body."

In other words, I would be lying on a table and letting this stranger put her hands on me until she feels she has a "solid understanding" of my body. I have enough experience with both evaluations and physical therapy to know that they are impossible to do in one hour and a waste of my time/money.

"Okay," I said anyway. I didn't know her well enough to fight back.

I transferred onto the table propped myself up on my elbows. Michelle seized my leg and started a familiar kicking motion I've been through so many times at home. While my legs were going through these motions, I was supposed to be visualizing the movement in my head and trying to make connections with the sensation.

Honestly I did try to think about it, but it was just very hard to concentrate with so many new things surrounding me. There was an attractive boy in the corner that had been staring at me ever since I rolled into the gym, and I was trying my hardest to make eye contact and give him my most charming smile. After all, it was Spring Break and I was a teenager. I should have been running around on a beach with my friends, but instead I was practicing floor-to-chair transfers in a rehab center in Ohio. I was desperate for a distraction.

Abandoning the small remainder of focus on my legs, I let my eyes wander to a man suspended in a harness over a treadmill, a recumbent bike in the corner, and another man walking across the gym using a walker and leg braces. The leg braces the last man was wearing, though, those were the coolest. I didn't find out a whole lot about them until I got home.

Everything was new to me and I was eager to try it all. It seemed ridiculous that I was lying on a table with a weird woman moving my legs in circles.

"We'll be doing that," Michelle nodded toward the man on the treadmill and said. "I don't know if we'll have time to try the bike because you're only here for a week, but we might be able to fit it in." I smiled across my face. Maybe SCI Step will be a good place after all.

I heard the front door breeze open and, from the corner of my eye, I saw a man walk in the facility. He danced straight across the hall and toward a set of closed doors.

"What's behind those doors?" I asked, still distracted.

"That's where we have acupuncture and massage therapy," Michelle said casually. As if massage therapy isn't the most exciting thing.

Like a dog after a bone, my mom swooped in from wherever she was standing and began asking questions.

"Acupuncture? How do you feel about that? Would you suggest we do it? We did it in California and liked it. Have you ever had it done?"

"Yes," Michelle shot back. "Acupuncture is awesome. I feel like it really does help. You should definitely give it a try. I can set you up a session with…"

Their conversation went on for another ten minutes and massage therapy wasn't mentioned again. I lost interest and blocked them out. Again, I was more interested in the boy in the corner. He wore a white t-shirt, surfer shorts and was surprisingly attractive. That's worth me reiterating. Now I caught myself staring at him while he was exercising – the tables turn.

"Okay," Michelle said, tearing me from my thoughts. "Get off this table and we'll put you in the harness."

She didn't say it, but I assumed that meant that I was going to walk over the treadmill like she teased earlier. I didn't exactly know what to expect as I hadn't walked over a treadmill in a harness before, but it didn't look like much of a challenge. It kind of looked like a do-it-yourself version of a gait trainer. From watching the man before me, it looked like my only job is to hold the handles and let the trainers move my legs in walking motion. It looked like all I had to do is hang there.

Michelle strapped me into the harness and I shuffled onto the machine.

It took me only two seconds to see how wrong I was. Hanging in a harness over a treadmill is not only uncomfortable because of its stiff costume, it also requires my complete effort and attention. As my legs move back and forth to imitate a walking movement, I have to stabilize my upper body to allow my lower body isolation in movement. If I don't do that, the movement from my lower body would thrash my upper body side to side in a very uncomfortable pattern. I learned that quickly.

Like all exercises, I also follow the movements in my head to imagine my body initiating and performing them. Again, the end goal is a stronger mind-body connection. That means that I had to watch the trainer-guided movement of my legs, visualize my body carrying them out on my own, and pay attention to any feelings or tingles I had during the movement. All of those things completely occupied my mind and I had to abandon my focus from possibly the only attractive boy in the state of Ohio.

"Okay," Michelle said abruptly. It seemed like everything she said was abrupt. She pounded buttons to stop the treadmill, raised her eyebrow, and looked at my body up and down like she was expecting me to get myself off the machine and walk away. "Our hour is over. You did a great job on this."

"Thank you," I said. "The treadmill was fun."

Honestly, it wasn't that fun – but it's practical. I'm grateful for any time I spend upright. On my feet again.

Mom saw that I was done with my workout and trotted up to us with a well-practiced smile across her face. For a few more minutes she and Michelle maintained a conversation that I chose not to listen to. I think they were talking about fun things to do in the town of Mason – a very short conversation. All we really needed was a grocery store and WiFi, and Mom knew that. All we really needed was a computer to play QBeez. It's the only computer game she'll play and just about the only fun thing to do in that state.

I'll be visiting Woodrow Wilson Rehab Center in Staunton, Virginia tomorrow to see if it will be a good fit for Kristin. This facility has equipment much like Ohio's SCI Step. They can also teach Kristin how to drive a hand-controlled car. Kristin is not excited about "yet another rehab place." Her little face got all distorted when we talked about it. "If I keep going to all these places, I won't have a life! I want some time to just be with my friends."

It looks like my social butterfly is getting an itchy trigger finger. I explained that this facility is not in addition to, but in place of another center. I think this calmed her down a little. Hopefully this facility will be a good match for us.

CHAPTER 6

Woodrow Wilson

woke abruptly to the distinct smell of diarrhea. I frantically checked myself to make sure I wasn't the source of the bad smell, always to find that it was the outside air.

Just as we would enter the mountain range, it would hit me: a smell strong enough to wake me from sleep. I went through this same routine every morning. The smell came at about the time we had twenty minutes left of our drive, so it also served as my wakeup call. The stench gave me no option of drifting back into sleep, so I straightened up to look outside.

I looked out the window at the "beautiful" mountains that lined the highway and felt nothing but dread. I hated those mountains. I hated them because of what they meant. Those mountains meant waking up at 6:00 every morning of the summer after my sophomore year in high school; driving 98 miles and almost two hours on a busy interstate; and arriving at Woodrow Wilson Rehabilitation Center by 8:30am. Every morning for six weeks.

> *Kristin has been going to Woodrow Wilson Rehab Center in Staunton, VA ever since returning to Richmond. Every morning, Rhonda and Kristin drive 1 hour and 40 minutes (each way) for a 2 hour workout. At WWRH, Kristin has been training for brace walking. The hip-high braces are a training tool to, hopefully, train those legs to walk again. Initially, the focus is on standing up and sitting down with the braces on. Next, she uses a walker to move both legs in tandem while putting weight on the walker. This takes a lot of upper body strength. She is essentially "hopping" with every movement forward. Kristin does not like the hopping move and feels absurd doing it. However, it is only the first phase of the total training.*

Despite the smell and dilapidating atmosphere of Staunton, VA, a tiny, tiny part of me didn't mind going to Woodrow Wilson so much. At Woodrow I had a chance to practice walking on my new and endlessly exciting leg braces. I saw someone using leg braces while I was in Ohio and, true to my Beale name, researched them and had an appointment to get some of my own a few months after returning home. That was the biggest, if not only, benefit I got from my week at SCI Step.

The braces looked like two plastic shields wrapped around each leg and reaching the top of my thigh. The ones I was using at Woodrow were loaners until I could get braces of my own, and they looked every second of 100 years old. They were templates made to fit every person who needed them in the gym, so they had to be universal to every body size. In my case, those leg braces weighted as much as me and swallowed my skinny legs. Cumbersome, to say the least.

The leg braces I was going to get, though, let me tell you. They were custom molded to every curve [or lack of curve] in my legs, and held together by three tight Velcro straps. There's a contraption set over my knee joints that prohibits them from bending, because that's beyond what I was capable of handling at that point. Eventually when I have the strength and nerve control to utilize muscles in my butt, thighs, quadriceps and calves, I'll be able to loosen the bond and walk with a normal, knee-bending gait; the leg braces served as a stepping stone toward my normalcy. Until I get to that point, though, my leg braces take care of me by keeping my knees locked. And until I got home, I was using the loaner braces.

Woodrow Wilson was my first encounter with walking after my accident; that place brought me closer than I had been to my goal. Not only was I lying in bed for almost 3 straight months, my doctors told me I would never be higher than a sitting position for the rest of my life. Until I got to Woodrow, I had accepted that fate. I accepted a lot of fates when I was in the hospital. I believed every dull prediction my doctors threw at me until I was discharged and saw how wrong they were. Disability isn't as black and white as they made me believe.

Try to imagine yourself at 15 years old being told that you'll never feel sensations again and will see the world from the height of a toddler for the next 75 years of your life, assuming we'll all live until 90. They weren't just saying that I'll be short, either. They were saying I would have to give up the sports I loved, all the sensations I've ever felt on my lower half, and even looking at people at eye level. Their predictions nearly destroyed me.

Another thing the doctors' forecasting did, though, is motivate me. The more I practice walking, locked knees or not, the more opportunity my body has to remember and carry out those movements without so much help. The hope from my leg braces and motivation from my naysaying doctors brought me to my first long term goal: walk across the stage at my high school graduation. You see? It's all very exciting.

Mom drove the car off the interstate and onto Tinkling Spring Road. I looked at the town surrounding us and made a small, pathetic giggle.

We were surrounded by Woodrow Wilson High School, Woodrow Wilson Middle School, and Woodrow Wilson Elementary School.

"What's funny?" Mom asked. She looked at me from across the car.

"Everything around here is named after Woodrow Wilson," I said. "That would be annoying."

"Well," she paused with reflection and probably a scramble for response. "He was a great man."

Her argument was weak but I didn't care enough to challenge, so I let her have it.

"You're right," I said. She deserved to win one.

Within few minutes we arrived at the rehab center. Even considering my opportunity to brace-walk, our arrival was always too soon. Mom jumped out of the car to get my wheelchair from the trunk in the same second of parking, and I reluctantly opened the door to swing my legs out. I transferred into my chair, pulled down my shirt, readjusted my pants over my legs, and sat up to look at the pale, grim atmosphere around me. I was moving as slowly as possible – I admit that.

Mom handed me my bag of leg braces, showed a strained smile, and turned to walk toward the entrance of the building. I followed her through two heavy, beige doors.

As soon as I rolled into the lobby, another smell hit me: rotten peanut butter mixed with the distinct odor of hairspray. I looked around at the bland decorations and colorless walls, and felt my heart sink. The room was filled with florescent lighting and a loud humming noise that made it hard to concentrate on anything else. The tile on the floor looked like it belonged in a nursing home from 1970, and the air had a sour, mildewed taste that coated my mouth and throat. I looked at Mom with a calloused expression on my face.

The waiting room of the lobby included six decrepit people sitting in brown, rusty chairs and looked like they might die at any moment. Most of them were asleep, but two were staring at the ground with glazed eyes, threatening to fall to the ground at any moment. It was like a scene of a nursing home horror story and I felt queasy.

In the center of the lobby, there was a head of hair behind a reception desk whom I had seen many times before, but never recognized. Without stopping my movement from the front door, I rolled past her to the elevator and repeatedly pressed the "Up" button – as if that would make it come any faster. I feared the smell of the lobby would attach itself to me and send me home smelling like diarrhea, peanut butter and hairspray.

The elevator dumped us in a skinny, brown hallway that opened up to the gym. I saw my therapist, Mabel, from across the room waving her moist hand and smiling with only two of her teeth. Like every morning, she nodded toward the blue mat.

I cooperated and wheeled over to park my chair at the mat's edge. Mom sat in front of me, grabbed my leg, and began to unpack and un-Velcro the straps on my leg braces. Three weeks of coming to Woodrow Wilson meant we were in routine of putting them on quickly and nearly thoughtlessly. I reached down and pulled the Velcro straps to tighten the plastic cones tightly around my thighs. Mom and I exchanged looks, not words.

When my legs were fully clothed in plastic bracing, we sat on the mat and waited for Mabel to finish with another client. Mom read the look of distaste I accidentally put on my face and touched me on the top of my left hand.

"What's wrong?" she asked, pretending to not already know.

I didn't have time to answer because Mabel walked up to us with a large, nauseating grin on her face. I think that was better than any answer I could have given.

"Are you ready to get started?" she spat. Literally spat. I wiped a bead of spit off my cheek.

"Yes," I answered and stared at her. In my mind I was screaming "NO."

"You look tired this morning," she observed in a failed attempt at conversation.

"Of course I'm tired," I thought. "Tired and unhappy."

I wanted to say that, but of course I had to be polite. I put on a well-practiced fake smile and nodded my head.

One of the 'unseen' side effects of a disabling accident is that you have to try to be understanding and polite to people who say all kinds of lame and sometimes annoying things. Often, people are already extra conscious of themselves when they're faced with unlikeness such as a wheelchair. The worst thing I could do is be impolite or insensitive, because that can easily create a negative generalization for other wheelchair users and people in similar situations. For that reason I put on a little bit of a show. Most of it is my natural personality, but sometimes it's forced. It's exhausting.

"I'll go get your walker," she said and pranced to the closet on the other side of the gym.

Mom and I sat in silence for the ten seconds it took her to appear back in front of me with my ancient loaner walker in her hands. She unfolded the rusted frame, set down the two bright yellow tennis balls on the front legs, and grazed her clammy fingers over the handles that were taped and covered in white washcloths to protect my hands from unforgiving grips.

Grudgingly, I grabbed them and pushed up until my body was in standing position.

Mom walked behind me and planted herself on a sofa at the other side of the room with a Southern Living magazine and her polka dotted reading glasses. In the beginning she would sit on the mat and chat with Mabel while I worked, but soon the conversation dried up and she started going to the corner to read. I understood.

"All right," Mabel blurted from behind me. "Let's go."

She stood ridiculously with her hands out and legs in a crouched position, ready to spot my first step. I used another fake smile and lifted the walker off the ground to plant two inches in front of me. My standing-balance, or lack thereof, was inept and I had to start small. I pushed with my arms so my legs hovered and my body floated forward to meet my walker. My feet dropped back onto the ground and my hips wobbled into balance.

"Good," I heard Mabel whisper, probably because she saw my struggle.

That rare acknowledgement was all the dialogue I wanted and all I would receive during my walks. We were long past the point of small talk and were not able to find common ground for conversation.

I repeated that hopping motion until I reached the silver mat on the opposite side of the gym. It felt like I had just brace-walked a 5k.

Even with my struggle, Woodrow Wilson is hard to take but so seriously because I was spoiled by California and Project Walk. At Woodrow, I was only working out my muscles – nobody seemed to get the clue of adding in my mind. In California I learned the right way to work out: building up that scar-tissue-bridge. I felt smarter than Mabel in this way.

"Okay," I said through heavy breaths. "I sit here."

My heavy breathing turned me into a caveman.

"All right." Mabel was cooperating with me now. The tables turn. "Just turn around and ease yourself down like we practiced."

My body was already in motion. I staggered my walker to the left, pushed my legs one inch off the ground, and let my body collapse backwards, only hoping it would land on the mat. I was too tired to use any of the sitting skills that I learned the day before, and was willing to sit through Mabel's inevitable lecture during my rest. As long as I could sit while I listened.

"Kristin you forgot to line your toes with the walker's legs," she fussed. "Remember what happens when you get sloppy – you get hurt."

She kept talking but her voice was in my background. My upper back burned sore from hunching over to the walker and my arms were burning from the extra effort to reach the short handles below. My loaner walker wasn't tall enough for my newly-lanky body, so I had to compromise. To everyone's surprise, my legs grew what seemed like three feet in the hospital and I now cast a shadow on anything I stand next to.

"Okay let's keep walking," Mabel sprinkled me with spit. "This is your last lap."

I stood back up and glanced at people doing similar exercises as me. I mumbled "hello" to some that had become familiar faces due to my working beside them every morning for nearly a month. As I inched across the floor, I very clearly felt a strain in my brow and grumpy expression on my face that I couldn't hide any longer.

"When you get to the mat it'll be time to go," Mabel repeated. A smile spread across my face – a smile I thought I was incapable of making. "Keep going."

I looked across the gym to Mom talking to a man I had never seen before. I saw a familiar excitement on her face as they spoke.

She felt me looking at her, glanced at the clock, and said what I think was "goodbye" to the man. At the end of my physical therapy sessions at Woodrow Wilson she was fully aware of my eagerness to go home, so she hopped up and sashayed over to the mat to wait and help take off my leg braces.

My walk back through the gym was the quickest. The incentive of leaving when I reached the blue mat meant I didn't use any of my stalling tactics on my still-naïve trainer Mabel. I didn't scratch my nose, stare at the clock, engage in conversation, or "reposition my hips." I just walked.

Mom met me at the mat to tag-team pulling off my braces and changing my shoes from Nike to Converse. In the same minute my legs were free from the braces, I turned to zoom out of the gym. That's when I noticed Mabel standing next to and too close to us.

"That was fun," I said with my last attempt at sincerity. "Thank you."

"See you tomorrow then," she responded with a small laugh. Surely she was aware of my falsity.

Even still, by the time she finished her response, I was already halfway to the door. My arms and upper back were tired and aching from my workout and I could only think of one thing: getting into the car and going home.

The trip back through the smelly lobby was not as unpleasant as the initial one since, by now, I was either used to the smell or had acquired the smell. Without hesitation I rolled straight for the double doors and into the fresh air of the world. Leaving Woodrow Wilson felt like I was breaking out of jail – a smelly, dusty jail with old people and parallel bars.

"I've got you," Mom chanted as she grabbed my handlebars and pushed my wheelchair through the parking lot. "You worked hard today. Good job."

I don't know how she knew that – she was sleeping the whole time.

"Thank you," I said, too tired to laugh.

We reached the trunk of her car and I took control of my wheelchair to push to the passenger door. Mom came behind me, grabbed the handles of my wheelchair once I was transferred out, and tossed it into the trunk.

"Did you see that man I was talking to?" Mom asked. "He was telling me about an adaptive skiing program at Wintergreen. Have you ever heard of that?"

"Adaptive skiing?" I asked, confirmed. "I haven't. That sounds like it could be fun. Snow is the worst, though."

"I think it would definitely be fun," Mom said with a raise of inflection. "I'll look into it." She turned to look me in my eyes. "He also gave me the name of a lady close to home who knows about brace walking: Tina."

Her voice was excited. I probably should have been more excited about it, but I was just exhausted.

"Okay," I said and sunk back into the car seat. I immediately felt myself drifting into sleep. I reclined the seat, closed my eyes, and allowed myself to relax into a doze as Mom drove us back home. After all, I had a hard workout.

CHAPTER 7

Skiing

Kristin has showed interest in the adaptive skiing program at Wintergreen. For the life of me, I don't see how they do it, but they're going to teach Kristin to snow ski! She is very excited. It's the first adaptive sport that she has been excited about doing. As you might imagine, the rest of us are feeling a little bit nervous about this, but we feel very confident in the people involved in the program. She was accepted in a grant program where she will be assigned a mentor, they will ski at Wintergreen, then the program will fund her trip to Breckenridge, Colorado for one week of skiing. It's really an incredible program.

"Which chair do you want?" a man in a Wintergreen vest trotted over to us and asked. His expression was bored and his voice monotone.

"Chair seven, please," I answered, feeling like a boss.

I raised my monoski into lift position and waited for my chair to arrive. The wind was frozen and I was happy to sit still for a minute. If nothing else, I was postponing the additional breeze from a ride up the ski lift of the Blue Ridge Mountains of Virginia.

My day started early with the familiar padding of my flat-footed mother hurrying across the marble foyer into my room to make sure I was out of bed.

Even though I was awake, I laid motionless with my eyes closed and the intention of tricking her into a few more moments of sleep. But, like every Saturday, she made it impossible for me to pretend by grabbing my feet and sliding my ski pants up my legs. I shamelessly accepted her babying, kept my eyes closed, and weakly shifted my weight to each side so she could pull the pants up to my waist.

"Okay," Mom said in a suddenly hurried tone. "Get up and put your shirt on. Come on let's get going. I don't want to be late again."

I moaned and sat up just in time to catch the long-underwear she chucked at me from across the room. With minimal words exchanged, I grabbed a granola bar for breakfast, brushed my teeth, and hustled through the door. Mom, Dad, and I were on the road in record time: 8:30am.

> *On the mornings we go to Wintergreen, it is very difficult to get her motivated. She says, "Dad, it's just like cheerleading. I would always dread going to practice but, once I got there, I loved it." This is obviously tougher than cheerleading practice because we have to leave so early and it's 1 1/2 hours away. It is a real plus to see her smile after a big run, though, so it's worth it.*

The ride to Wintergreen is always a quiet, comfortable one. Mom sits in the back seat sleeping, I am slowly waking up, and Dad is behind the wheel with only the sound of the highway passing underneath us. That never lasted long, though – only about 20 minutes actually. Dad would soon get bored and start to pick at me until I talk to him.

"What are you doing?" he quietly yelled. His hand reached over and laid limply on my shoulder.

"Dad," I said as firmly and believably as I could. I couldn't make eye contact because he would see the smile I tried to hide. "No Dead Hand. You can't start that."

"I don't know what you're talking about," he said and repositioned the Dead Hand closer to my neck.

For the rest of the ride Dad stuck his finger in my ear, quiet-screamed messages from across the car, patted me on the head and, worst of all, rested his limp hand ("Dead Hand") on my shoulder and against my neck.

At the end of 2 hours we arrived at the top of the mountain. Dad pulled in front of the Adaptive Ski Hut next to the uppermost ski lift, and our car finally stopped moving.

"Wake up, Mama," Dad burst as soon as we were still. "We're here."

Mom's eyes popped open and she sprang into action: the crinkle of wrappers from her bag of snacks, the soft groan of putting on her jacket, and a small collapse of ski supplies falling onto the seat. Dad pulled my wheelchair to me from the trunk and I transferred out of the car without a word. He dropped my bag of ski accessories into my lap and I rolled across the gravel parking lot to the door of the hut. We had our routine.

Immediately after I turned the handle to open the hut's door, I was welcomed by familiar and endearingly rambunctious yells from a crowd of people inside.

"HELLO BEALE FAMILY," an instructor yelled at us in an almost aggressive tone. His greeting was followed by a howl and few claps. The four other people in the small hut were smiling and cheering at us. It made us feel like stars. Me, at least.

Despite the cold weather and wind speeds that made my snot touch the corner of my mouth, these people could and did erupt with energy at all times of the day. It's amazing to see so many people give up their Saturdays to help people with physical and mental disabilities have fun in the snow. Everyone on staff has a constantly joyful mood that makes it obvious they love what they're doing and genuinely wanted to be there. Their energy was infectious and made accommodating my disability not seem like so much of a drag.

"Wake up," shouted my extremely attractive instructor, Tobey, when he saw me come in the door. "They blew snow last night so today should be really good."

Without fail, a smile spread all the way across my face. With motivation of freshly-blown snow and a good looking man, I floated over to my ski bag and got my body ready for the snow. That means a winter jacket, 2 pair of long pants plus coveralls to protect low-circulating legs, gloves with mittens on top, knee high socks, snow boots, and warmers for my toes and fingers. I was a sight.

Winters at Wintergreen are tricky; it's rare for enough natural snow to fall on the slopes to make it all the way to the bottom of the hill on skis or a snowboard. The biggest obstacle I face is not to stay upright on my monoski, but to avoid the muddy, rocky areas that cover a large percentage of the hill. The rock-obstacles added an extra challenge to the skiing, making adaptive skiing more demanding than it already is. I'm not saying I conquered or even successfully completed the avoidance challenge, but I at least accepted the challenge.

"Is everyone ready?" I shouted to the hut. I locked eyes with Tobey in the creepiest way possible. "I'm ready to go."

I looked out of the small window and felt an adrenaline fill my body. The sight of face-planting children, iced ski lifts, and man-made snowflakes did nothing but confirm my love for the sport. Besides the obvious losses I took with my paralysis, my inability to participate in sports was the most significant. Adaptive skiing was the first on a long and growing list of adaptive sports I've tried. It was a stepping stone to therapeutic and rehabilitative benefits that sports provided after my accident.

I zipped my jacket to my neck, grabbed a carabiner and a handful of things I had seen hanging out of Tobey's pockets, and pointed my wheelchair toward the door.

"Yeah," Tobey shouted back to me. "We're waiting on you."

He walked over and grabbed the door knob with his left hand and hugged his snowboard close to his chest with his right. I gave my most charming-feeling smile, rolled past him through the door, down the crooked ramp, and parked my chair next to a golf cart at the bottom.

"HEYO," Michael shouted when he saw me rolling toward him. "LET'S GO SKIING."

"I'M READY" I shouted back, matching his enthusiasm. Remember: it's infectious.

Michael is the director and the most fun part of the program. He's a grey haired, energetic man that is always able to make me laugh, even if just from looking at him. Per Michael's handiwork, the golf cart was decorated with gaudy beads, horns, and streamers to assure that everyone we pass on our way to the top of the slope is paying attention. To further ensure we have everyone's attention, Michael honks a horn a couple hundred times followed by an animalistic howl. Seriously every time.

My and Tobey's gear was already loaded onto the cart, so we were ready to go as soon as our bodies were loaded in.

"HERE WE GO," Michael announced to the left side of the mountain. With another honk and a scream, he drove us up the slope and didn't stop until we reached the ski lift.

"Okay," said Tobey, too soon. "C'mon. We can get out here and get you on your ski."

Sometimes I got so caught up in the fun of the golf cart ride, I would almost just prefer to ride it around and beep the horn with Michael.

"All right," I said without hesitation. A good looking man doesn't have to tell me twice to follow him. "Let's do this."

With a small amount of Tobey's help, I transferred out of the cart, loaded myself into the bucket seat of my monoski, and strapped my legs into the footplate. My energy was still untapped and my movements were still relatively effortless and smooth, so it was okay. With attractive Tobey by my side and a dry jacket on my chest, I was feeling good.

The monoski I use is a simple but also complicated contraption: simple once you get used to it, but looks impossible at first glance. My body sits in a bucket-like seat perched on a single ski with a footplate in front that my legs are tightly strapped into. My knees bend at 40°, forcing my body into an "athletic position." I change direction and stabilize myself using two outriggers made of 3 foot adjustable poles with 30 inch mini skis attached to the bottom. My posture is horribly uncomfortable and silly looking when I'm sitting still, but everything works together to help me balance while I ski.

"Get ready to go," shouted Tobey from behind me.

"I'm ready," I shouted back. "Okay."

I felt his hands on my back giving my monoski a small shove and I shot across the hill at top speed.

The upper half of the slope, called the "Bunny Slope," is crowded with little kids, families, and ski classes. In honest words, the top of the hill is where you find the underdeveloped, idiotic children jumping in front of your ski like they're making a sacrifice. In anticipation of those kids jumping in front and flailing their bodies, traffic on the Bunny Slope is always slow. I'm relatively inexperienced at skiing and kids, so my avoidance skills are nonexistent; several times I've lost control, collided with a small body, and nosedived into the snow. I felt guilty at first but, as we became better friends, the instructors clued me in on a game they play – unofficially called "Knock Down Anyone Who Gets In Your Way." I don't think they meant it to be literal, but that's how I took it. I was winning the game.

The end of the Bunny Slope is where my real fun begins. When I finally make it to that point, the slope is usually almost empty and my anticipation is overflowing. At this position on the top of the hill,

I could barely see the [mud and rock filled] bottom and it was hard to picture the slope being anything but perfect.

"All right girl," I heard Tobey say from behind me. "Here we go."

I nodded my neckless head and pointed my ski downhill. My ski picked up speed faster than I expected and an overwhelming feeling of freedom and absolution came over me that I showed with a goofy looking smile spread across my face. Thankfully no one was in front of me to see it. That part of the slope is less populated, meaning I can ski faster and more carelessly. That's exactly what I intended to do.

In my monoski, I have an opportunity to be in the world without my wheelchair and while doing an impressive-looking skill, regardless of how successful I am at it. People look at me with curiosity and sometimes even awe, instead of charity and what sometimes feels like superiority. I'll take any opportunity I can to show up in a vehicle other than my wheelchair, and a monoski was a great option.

Before I could finish my thought or comprehend what was happening, my vision was taken by a white mass of nothing. It all happened so fast I had to lie in the snow for a moment before pulling my face out of the frigid cold. The extra seconds I took to register my circumstance cost me all feeling and color in my face; I was numb, red, and swollen. I looked up and saw the backside of a purple jacket climbing up from the ground to ski away. I was in more shock than I was in pain.

"That was her fault," I said to no one. My face was swollen so my words were coming out in slur. "Her fault."

"One hundred percent," Tobey shouted from behind me.

I didn't know he could hear me but I'm so glad he did. It's easy to blame another person when they're not around to defend themselves, and even better is if I can get someone else to agree with me.

I put my hand to my face and realized a string of drool from the side of my mouth. I slurped it back and turned to look uphill at Tobey snowboarding toward me to help lift my body back into my ski. I repositioned myself and smiled as sweetly as I could, trying to trick him into thinking I was cute and attractive.

"I'll help you," he shouted over the cold air and wind. "I don't want you to use all your energy getting up."

Praise the Lord. Tobey and his snowboard skied next to me and to my rescue. He bent down to grab onto silver bar on the side of my bucket, then froze in place. His two attractive eyes looked at me expectantly. I guess this was where I show him I'll help lift. I guess?

"Ready," he shouted. "1…2…3."

Tobey lunged forward for momentum then rocked his body weight back with my ski in his hands. His mouth let out a loud grunt that I'll never forget.

Pushing a monoski up from the ground requires me to partially unhook my outriggers from around my arm, dig my hands in the snow underneath my side, push my body weight upwards until I'm high enough to reach my other outrigger, swing my body around to grab its handle, then push my body and ski into a sitting position. It was hard work, to say the least. It's also the worst part of adaptive skiing. I wasn't going to refuse some help, no way.

My already-fatigued upper body only allowed me to initiate the push and let Tobey finish it off. I'm sure to fix my face with a furrowed brow and troubled expression so he thinks I'm straining with a lot of effort but, in reality, I'm not at all; all I do is hold my outriggers and nudge my ski with a baby's arms. That is my secret. I used to feel guilty because of the grunts and moans that came from my lifters, but the cold air and icy snow helped me get over my guilt pretty fast.

Once I was sitting up in my ski and without another word, I turned around and continued down the hill. With Tobey at my immediate left, I glided down the remainder of the hill without falling again.

Not soon enough, we reached the bottom of the hill and to my favorite part: the ski lift. Students in the Adaptive Ski program are allowed to advance to the front and past everyone else's shivering bodies in the lift line. With a grain of superiority, I propelled myself and my ski past the people to our special spot in the front.

People didn't act bitter about it like I expected them to, either. Instead they looked at me with eyes of unnecessary pity—I think because I use a sit-ski. Little did they know, I was the happiest skier on the slopes. My situation may sometimes appear less fortunate or deserving of empathy, but I have the happiest life of anyone I know. There's no time to count losses.

"Chair number," a different man in a Wintergreen vest slid up to us and demanded.

"Ten," I shouted back.

I lost the ability for additional polite words like "please" and "thank you" at the same time I lost the color from my fingertips. I gave him all I had with that one word.

I watched as he held up ten gloved fingers to a lady behind the controllers. She nodded her head in agreement. I sat, waited, and rested in my uncomfortable ski while the skiers around me loaded onto the lift. The freezing air turned my surroundings and body numb. It felt like I was watching a movie.

Chair nine approached, the passageway was cleared, and people next in line stopped for me. I looked over to nod to them in thanks and was returned with some head nods and understanding expressions that said "it's okay, little girl. We understand." Little did they know.

"Okay," Tobey spoke for the first time since we arrived. "That's chair nine. Let's get ready."

I pushed myself to the edge of the loading zone and looked at his attractive face. Again, I smiled my most charming.

My outriggers were close beside me and my elbows were in the air at a 90° angle. L-shaped arms allowed few more inches to my push, and I needed every inch. Still, I looked silly.

The chair came and I timed my lift perfectly. My L's lifted my ski from the ground at the same moment the chair tapped the back of my bucket, allowing my bucket to slide onto the lift chair like a smear of mayonnaise. As precaution, Tobey grabbed my silver handle and pulled the ski to the back of the seat. I lowered the silver handlebar in front of us and we were a great team. I had worked hard all season to master independence loading onto the chair lift and I finally mastered it. I felt proud of myself and, again, showed it with a doofy smile on my face.

We rode up the hill in silence because I didn't have the energy to shout over the sound of the wind. As promised, the breeze froze the snot on my face and cast a red shadow around my eyes. Still, though, the ski lift is the best part of skiing.

"Let's meet on the snow over there," Tobey pointed his finger and said as our chair neared the top of the hill.

Except for small laughter from watching people fall into the snow below us, the ski lift ride was spent in relative silence. Not because Tobey is uninteresting and/or he wouldn't *ask me to be his girlfriend*, but because I was tired from skiing – mostly falling.

We reached the top of the hill and I unloaded with a fairly simple process: swing both outriggers and body weight forward with enough momentum that my ski slides off the seat and evenly onto the snow without falls. After that success, I glided to a vacant patch of snow to wait for Tobey to reassemble his snowboard.

"That was a good run," he looked up to me and said.

"Except for the wipeout," I mumbled. Success means no wipeouts and I wasn't about to let that one slide.

"Don't be hard on yourself," Tobey said back. "That was no big deal. Let's go again."

I nodded my head and turned my ski to point downhill. Tobey snowboarded to my side, smiled at me like my *soon-to-be boyfriend*, then we took off down the hill again.

Tobey and I skied for another hour until it was time for lunch. Unloading from the lift, we moved toward the middle of the Bunny Slope to the Wintergreen Adaptive Skiing meeting spot. This is where we were told to sit and wait for Michael to pick us up in the golf cart and carry us back to the hut. My body felt successfully fatigued and a lunch break was welcomed.

Right before we got off the ski lift for the last time, Tobey called on the walkie talkie for a ride back to the hut. Within 2 minutes of arriving at the meeting spot, we heard the sound of a horn and tires against the rocky, uneven earth. Then came the horn four more times and an animal-like scream, confirming that Michael was driving.

"Did you two have fun?" Michael asked in an almost-scream as soon as he got within earshot. He turned to look me in the eyes. "How did you do today?"

"She did great," Tobey said without making eye contact with anyone. I was grateful for him answering questions so I wouldn't have to move my tired mouth. "Only a few falls."

I think he answered so quickly so I wouldn't have the chance to negatively self-report again. The rest I got from not having to use my mouth-energy outweighed listening to Tobey's exaggerations, so I let it happen.

I fell to the back of the cart's seat and started to feel my body again: my hands burning red, my drooling mouth, and my sore upper back. In the distance I saw Mom and Dad standing outside the hut with my wheelchair. Like every Saturday, they were waiting to take me to lunch—the best parents.

I got to see Kristin skiing at Wintergreen today. The determined look on her face as she was coming down the hill was very cool. But the most rewarding part of this whole experience is to see a smile come on her face at the bottom of the hill in the lift line. What an absolute flow of emotion to see her work so hard to stay up going down the hill, and then see her feel so good about herself at the end of the run.

A friend/employee summed it all up perfectly after I described Kristin's skiing and how motivating it is. She said, "There are some things you just can't buy." That is such a true statement. There is almost nothing better than seeing a loved one come from behind, charge an obstacle with no reluctance, climb the mountain, "take the bull by the horns", etc. Kristin is an inspiration and a reminder to "live for the day"; take all that God is giving you and leave no opportunity untried.

Michael jumped into the driver's seat, honked the horn, and let out one more screech before driving us back to the hut. He was talking and laughing at 20 miles per hour, but I was too tired to hear his words. My body would only allow a weak laugh that was swallowed by the sound of jangling beads and the golf cart on the rocky ground.

The feeling of fatigue in my muscles and weakness of my mind makes me feel like I am home in my able body. Those are the same feelings I used to feel after 4-hour-long field hockey camp or a 2 hour-long competition cheerleading practice where we ran through the routine at least 30 times. I will do almost anything to feel that again. The feeling that my body is disarmed after I drive myself as hard as I can, and when it throbs like it has a second heartbeat. I didn't think there's a sport that will give me back that feeling, but adaptive skiing got close.

CHAPTER 8

Wounded Warrior

After such a good day Thursday, I had high expectations of Friday. I woke up in a great mood and was finally starting to enjoy adaptive skiing on the slopes of Breckenridge, Colorado. For what felt like the first time, I was looking forward to sitting in my monoski and pouring down the freshly snow-covered hills.

I looked out of the window to the ski lift, though, and my spirits were squashed. Snow was falling from a completely white sky and it was falling harder and thicker than I had ever seen snow fall in Virginia. In fact, I was in Colorado on a grant program with a group of 5-6 people from Wintergreen, so I probably wasn't alone in that naivety. Virginia doesn't get snow accumulations even in the same ballpark as Colorado.

I let out an audible moan and Mom came to stand next to me.

"It's going to be a bad day," I mumbled with bitterness pouring from my every word.

"It's snowing," she said with forced enthusiasm. "The slopes are covered in fresh powder."

I knew better than to rejoice at this. There will be fresh snow, but it'll be flying at my face and into my eyeballs while I ski down the hill. My face will become numb and my upper back will tense into an angry ball. The imagery is drawn up shoulders, an unrecognized stream of snot running from my nose into my mouth, and my strained expression of contentment.

I encased my body in 3 layers of shirts, a sweatshirt, winter jacket, two pairs of pants, two pair of gloves, a hat, and earmuffs. I looked like I was dressed for a comedy show. I followed Mom down the hall and to the elevator toward the Adaptive Ski Meeting Room.

We have been in Breckenridge, Colorado for the Hartford Ski Spectacular since this past Sunday. This week is where disabled skiers from all over the country convene to celebrate their ability to overcome some of the most difficult challenges and enjoy snow skiing. The Wounded Warriors are here in great numbers. There are so many amputees and other wounded men and women that have taken their situation in life in stride. Mono-skiers, like Kristin, are everywhere. Funny thing is that most of the mono-skiers and amputee skiers are faster than able-bodied skiers! They have no fear.

"It's 25 degrees outside and snowing," my ski instructor, Steven, walked from behind us and announced as soon as we appeared in the door of the small conference room. He motioned toward my monoski laying on its side in the corner.

He pointed, I think, to command me to transfer onto my ski so we could get moving toward the snow. I figured out that much, but I still acted oblivious. Yes, I was stalling. Every second of hotel-heat counts.

"We're going to wrap you up in a sleeping bag again today," he said. His voice was proud.

I looked at Mom and a tiny smile arrived on my face. The temperature yesterday was also painfully low, so Steven came up with a solution: ski in a sleeping bag. It sounded ridiculous but I'm definitely not one to shy away from an out-of-the-box suggestion. Actually, I was ready to try anything for an extra morsel of warmth.

Steven pulled a sleeping bag off a nearby table and tossed it onto my lap.

"Thank you," I said with a wide smile. Before I go out into the snow I tend to exaggerate my happiness – probably in anticipation of the snow sucking it out of me like a vacuum. Sitting in the heated lobby of the hotel, my words all end in exclamations and my face is a bubble. I looked at Steven like the sleeping bag was the greatest present I've ever received.

Mom snatched the bag from my lap, I pushed up on my wheels, and she helped me slide it up to swallow my body. Once the bag was fully around me, I sat in my wheelchair with my arms, shoulders, and head as the only body parts visible. It had to be funny looking.

Steven's justification behind the sleeping bag is to block out all cold air from my legs and feet to prevent damage from the cold air, such as frostbite or snow-white ankles. Rolling around in a sleeping bag had to be very silly looking, and that's another advantage.

"Are you ready to go?" Steven asked with unconscionable enthusiasm. I looked at him with wide eyes and a slightly open mouth. "I'm taking that as a yes. See you for lunch, Mom."

He grabbed the handle on the back of my monoski bucket and pushed through the door. Once again, I was a princess.

Almost as soon as we reached the snow, Steven let go of my ski and I was on my own. My performance the day before was so great that we both had a false confidence in my ability to stay afloat on a monoski. The falsity of our confidence was confirmed seconds later when my ski tipped over and my face crammed into the snow.

And the pattern continued: ski for 20 feet, loose control, face-plant.

After my forth time falling in five minutes, I was frustrated. One look at my face and Steven could tell exactly what I was feeling. I guess I'm not very good at hiding emotions.

"Why are you frustrated?" he asked and skied next to my puny body lying on the ground.

"I've fallen four times in the time it takes to brush my teeth," I said with a furrowed brow. My voice sounded extra high pitched for some reason.

"I'll tell you why," he responded calmly. "I'm giving you a lot less support than I usually do, and even letting you off tether sometimes." He grabbed my outrigger from behind him and yanked strap on my bucket to pull me upright. "It's OK to fall, Kristin. You just have to get used to it."

"Okay," I said with an immediate and slight increase in my confidence. I had never skied without a tether before. It was exciting. "Let's go again."

I turned my ski to direct down the never-endingly long slope and started to inch forward. Steven was 10 feet to my left – no tether.

Good news: Through the Wintergreen Adaptive Ski Program three year grant, Kristin is now skiing independently. Over the past 2 years, Kristin has been "on tether" with an instructor behind her – using the tether to control her speed, etc. Now, in Colorado's real snow and advanced slopes, she's doing it on her own!

Kristin keeps getting things thrown in her path making an already difficult situation worse. It reminds me of action movies where the bad guys throw things out the back of a truck in a highway chase to make the police crash. Kristin seems to be constantly dodging whatever comes at her and does it with a persistence I've never seen.

One day, all of this won't matter. Her body will be healed and we'll all be smiling. Life here is short; she's making the best of it.

The next hour and a half was filled with 100 yard victories, anticipated rides up the ski lift, and a nose repeatedly packed with snow. Most importantly, though, I was doing it on my own. I call that a victory.

At the top of the hill after our third run, we stopped to take a break and reevaluate the afternoon. Finally able to sit still, I immediately became aware of the ten throbbing fingers in my gloves.

"Oh my gosh," I said when I uncovered my fingers and saw that the tips were as white as the snow beneath me. Ten vanilla popsicles stuck out of 2 angry, red palms of my hands. Steven heard me and skied down to look over my shoulder. I continued. "Fingers pain. Hurts when move. So painful."

I spoke in sentence fragments because I couldn't feel my lips forming the words.

"Let's go inside," Steven said without two seconds' hesitation. I think he was looking for an excuse to go inside and I finally gave him one. It was just too cold.

Like the days before, Mom and Dad were waiting for me next to the door of the ski slope attached to the hotel. Mom had blankets stacked to her chin and Dad had my wheelchair and a dry jacket. I saw them standing there when I turned my ski around the corner and onto the hotel's property on the ski slope. Steven must have tipped someone off that we were coming inside because they were ready to wrap me in a blanket-cocoon and take me back to our room.

Rhonda and I stood and watched Kristin come down the mountain one particular afternoon. She carefully went from side to side of the slope and then headed straight down at a pretty good clip. "No fear" has become Kristin's motto as well. All bundled up, it's hard to see if she's having a good time. When she pulled up to us, I didn't even need to see her mouth. I could see a big smile in her eyes. Skiing has given her back her athleticism.

Her accident may have taken her legs away, but there is nothing that can change her spirit.

"Hi sweetie," Mom shouted when I slid in close to her. She bounced over to me and Dad followed closely in her trail. She pushed my wheelchair next to my ski and I made a smooth transfer into my seat. I felt someone's hands touching my butt to help my transfer, so that's probably why it was so easy. Whether it was an angel or one of my parents, I was grateful. Everyone needs their butt touched every once in a while.

"She did great today," Steven reported. He looked at me nodded his head, acknowledging that I was sitting on my fingers to warm them. "We came in early because her fingers hurt."

"Let's go back to the room and you can take a shower," Mom looked at me and said. She shook her head up and down to confirm.

I looked at her with wide eyes, mouthed a "thank you" to Steven, and pushed toward the elevator without a word. My face was too cold for words.

Not uncommon of Breckenridge's Wounded Warrior Ski Spectacular, we passed several veteran amputees on the way back to our hotel room. The atmosphere of strangers and the warmth of the hotel gave me a new streak of energy.

"I've never seen a wheelchair the same color as mine," I said when I was in earshot of an amputee rolling toward me. He sat in a toxic green chair that could be seen from the other side of the building.

"Toxic green," he shouted energetically from 100 feet away. He rolled to us and stopped for conversation. "Are you a vet?" His eyes scanned my body and his tone was suspicious.

"No I'm not," I said.

I had been asked this question so much in the past 5 days that I considered answering with "yes" and telling a pretend story from my chronicles of a teenaged war veteran. That would be fun but it also would be a lie.

"I just got back from South Baghdad three months ago," he explained and motioned toward his lower body. "I stepped on a land mine and my legs flew off." Pause to look at our reactions. "I want to go back as soon as they'll let me."

"What was the best part about it?" I asked, surprised by his directness and feeling extra comfortable in the warmth of the hotel.

"I remember one day specifically," he began. "We were attacking a village and the lieutenant told us that we had open fire. He said there are no boundaries, just blow. That was definitely the most fun day."

"Oh my gosh," I heard Mom in a hushed voice.

"We literally had to kill everyone we saw," he continued. "It was crazy because everyone was bad; there were women and children walking around the village with explosives strapped to their chests."

I listened to him and couldn't help but draw on the differences between me and him: my fun is a computer game and a cookie, and his fun is blowing the heads off of foreigners.

We talked to the man for a few more minutes about, honestly, I don't know. I was so tired that I must have zoned out.

"Well," Dad said. I came back to attention with his voice. "I appreciate what you did for our country. Thank you."

I looked at my watch and saw that we had been standing there for 20 minutes – we had lost track of time talking to this guy. I became aware of how exhausted and dirty my body was and hoped other people hadn't noticed that, too. I looked at Mom and gave her a tiny nod that meant I was ready to go: our unspoken language.

"It was really great to meet you," Mom said in a polite but finalizing voice. "We'll see you at the closing banquet."

Without a pause, he gave us a military salute and rolled on. Mom, Dad, and I continued on the journey to our hotel room. Taking a shower was my only priority.

As soon as I took a shower and changed into my pajamas, I plopped myself on the couch between my parents. Finally able to relax for the first time after my day of skiing, all the exhaustion and fatigue resurfaced and smacked me in the face. Dad ordered room service, Mom squeezed us under a giant blanket, and a nameless sitcom played on the TV.

The show ended and Mom wasted no time before jumping off the couch and scrambling around the room. Dad and I got sleepier as time passed, but it's like she drank a cup of espresso. Where did that energy come from?

"Okay guys," she said. "We should get to bed. You have a big day tomorrow, girlfriend." She clapped her hands once in front of my face.

"Okay," I said in a normal-volume voice this time. Sometimes it's a bummer to have to transfer into my wheelchair after being somewhere comfortable like a sofa.

I dragged myself to the bathroom to brush my teeth and slumped deep under the covers. I was exhausted. I laid in bed and talked to God quickly before I let myself fall asleep. I asked for a better day tomorrow. More specifically I asked for the snow to stop falling overnight, the temperature to rise, and for me to be a better skier by morning. That would be great. Either that, or if it wouldn't hurt so badly when I fall.

CHAPTER 9

Dog Sledding

The end of the day at the end of the week of my vacation to Breckenridge, Colorado meant my body was haggard and fatigued after a week of face plants, snow-packed nostrils, and minute-long successes on the monoski I used for adaptive skiing.

In the evening after my final afternoon ski session, I was a zombie following Mom and Dad away from the Wintergreen Adaptive Sports meeting room toward our hotel room. The hotel was huge and the hallways were long, so it was less of an errand and more of a voyage.

"Let's stop here," Mom said when we arrived in front of the lobby. "I want to look at this."

She walked toward the wall of brochures and pulled one off the wall. I rolled closer and saw advertisement for a shopping center in town. Dad was looking at something with his back to us and I was in a tired-trance, so I sunk down in my chair behind them to wait.

"This would be fun," Dad said.

He spun around and I saw in his hands a brochure with the words "Dog Sledding" printed on the front. He flipped through the booklet and stared at its contents for one minute.

"Do you guys want to try it?" he asked me and Mom.

Of course the answer is yes.

"That would be cool," I responded energetically. Mom gave a soft smile and nodded her head.

"That would be fun," she whispered.

She walked over to the wall of brochures and picked up the same one. Dad was already talking to a woman behind the concierge desk. He appeared back in front of us minutes later.

"I made a reservation for tomorrow morning," he proudly announced. "A van will pick us up at 9am in the lobby."

Mom, Dad, and I stood in a small circle and smiled excitement at each other for another minute before leaving the lobby and continuing the trip toward our hotel room. It was kind of a weird way to express our excitement, but we were just all very tired.

The next morning came quicker than it should have. We fell asleep almost immediately after getting back to our room – cold weather is draining. Snow was falling harder and thicker than it had the days before; Saturday morning's snowstorm was bigger than even Tuesday and Wednesday's snowstorm.

"You have to dress warm today," Mom said to me after breakfast. She told me the same thing every morning using a voice that sounded like she was saying something new and groundbreaking. "Wear this sweatshirt under your jacket."

She threw a black sweatshirt at my head. With that addition, my Colorado-snow-uniform included a sports bra, camisole shirt, short sleeved "sweat proof" shirt, long sleeved long underwear, a crewneck sweatshirt, and a three-inch-thick winter jacket. Add leggings, marshmallow pants, winter gloves, and a beanie and I could jelly roll down the hill without even needing a ski.

Mom and Dad were dressed in dramatically less clothes than me: jeans and light sweatshirts on both of them. My brain injury caused bad circulation and an increased danger of frostbite, so at least my dramatic appearance was justified. Still, the difference in our costumes made me look even more ridiculous as I rolled down the never-ending hallway toward the lobby.

"Beale," we heard a man shout in the air from the coldest part of the lobby.

I turned around and saw a short, Hispanic man swaying on his feet next to the sliding doors. He saw my gaze and started nodding his head up, down, and very quickly toward me. I didn't know what to do.

"That's us," Dad stepped forward and announced.

The man's face lit up like he had just won something. He raised his arms to swim around in the air above his head until his finger landed on a rusty van parked in the hotel entrance. With a nod of Dad's head, the three of us shuffled past him and slid through the hotel doors.

We approached the rusty van and Dad stepped forward to pull the door open, revealing a seat that was 4 feet off the ground. This van reminded me of the church vans that carried me and my youth group to retreats, amusement parks, and conferences – except this van was 100 years older.

"Let me help," Dad turned to me and offered. He opened his arms, swooped down to my body, picked me up, and set me on the seat. Our transition was smooth.

"PANDA BEARS," our driver shouted.

That's what it sounded like he said. He had a heavy accent and, of course, only talked in Spanish. We had to just ignore him.

Mom and Dad climbed into the car after me, the driver started the engine, and we slid out of the hotel's parking lot.

Our driver was really bad at driving. Added to the fact that buckets of snow were dumping on our windshield and ice was freezing on the roads, he was bad at driving. I can't emphasize that enough. The road was icy, he [seemingly] ignored every speed limit, my hands were numb because of the cold, and my knuckles were white from my grip on the van's door handle. I looked around and wondered if those seconds would be my last.

He finally slammed on the brakes and I almost flew from my seat. I would have, if not for my door-handle-death-grip. I felt the traction of the van's tires give out from under us and we slid probably one inch, felt like 10 inches, until we came to a stop. The very moment I felt like it was safe to let go, I flung the door open – breathing like a fish out of water.

Outside of the swampy van window I could only barely discern the outline of a house; the snow was dense and difficult to see through. Even so, I was anxious to get out of the van and out of range of our lunatic driver. I lifted my legs and faced them toward the door, as if that would make a difference. I wasn't going anywhere without Dad's lift.

"We're here," I moaned. Just to get everyone moving.

Looking ahead of me, I saw the snow had accumulated to touch the footplate of the van door – bad news for a wheelchair user. In my anticipation, the snow would reach the seat of my wheelchair, rendering my wheels useless and independence null. I was not excited about that.

"I'll help," I heard Dad's voice say, muted by the sound of the snowfall.

Faster than I thought was possible he appeared at my door, he lifted me from the car seat, and set my marshmallowed body into my wheelchair that Mom had already positioned next to the van. I was a princess.

"I have our bags," Mom whispered and trailed behind with our extra snow gear overflowing from her arms.

As soon as I could because I was cold, I turned my chair around and Dad pushed it in a wheelie through the snow and to the threshold of the small, dimly-lit cottage door. As soon as Mom opened the door, the cottage's warm air smacked me in my chapped face. It was fantastic.

"What time I pick up?" our van driver busted through the threshold and shouted to us with an accent I could barely understand. I didn't realize how bad his English was until he said that because we hadn't spoken but a few words to each other.

Dad turned to look at Mom.

"What do you think?" he asked, as if she had any idea.

"Come get them in two hours," a deep voice thundered from behind us. "The dogs can only run for an hour. Then they can come back here and drink hot chocolate."

I turned toward the voice and saw a hairy, overweight man wearing a plaid shirt sitting next to a fire. To his right was a young Asian couple holding a large camera and wide smiles on their faces. Stereotypes are fun.

Our driver looked at Dad in the eyes, shook his head up and down quickly, and turned on his heels.

"Two hour," shouted the back of his head. He shot out of the door into the snow.

"My name is Tom," the voice by the fire said. He looked each of the five of us in our eyes slowly, deliberately. "I'm in charge of this place. I'm going to take all of you out in two groups."

Tom turned to face only the three Beales. Again, the drama.

"You guys are going first," he continued. "I'll show you the dogs then we can get our team and go sledding."

"Oh we get to meet the dogs," Mom's tiny voice whispered from behind me. "Good."

"Do you guys want to meet the dogs?" Tom stood up and asked us. He didn't hear Mom's whisper. Maybe I'm the only one who hears Mom's whispers.

"That would be good," she said at an audible volume this time.

Tom stood from his chair and hobbled over to the coat rack.

"It's very cold out there," he said. "This is a big snow storm."

The three of us waited and watched Tom as he zipped, snapped, and buttoned the fastenings on his sizable winter jacket, also plaid. He walked from the coat rack to a table in the corner, grabbed a pair of overstuffed mittens and beanie from a drawer, and opened the thick door leading outside. The Chinese couple was sitting in the corner of the cabin talking and laughing with language I couldn't understand.

"I'll pull the sled in front of the door," he shouted from the back of his head. "Sit here and look out for me."

We stood outside and waited for Tom for only five minutes until he pulled in front of us on a 6 passenger snow mobile. Those five minutes felt like one hour with snow dust blowing in your face and snot dripping to your chin.

"Load yourselves on here," he shouted over the noise of the snowfall. "I'll take you to see the dogs. Then we can start."

With more ease than last time, Dad swooped my heavily-padded body onto the back seat of the snow mobile. Mom was right behind us, shuffling her own body onto the vehicle as quickly as possible. Everything was done as quickly as possible with hopes that either movement of getting to or arriving at the next destination would bring our bodies more warmth.

"Are you comfortable?" Dad asked at the top of his voice.

I nodded my head and gave him a thumbs up. Multiple layers of clothing made my neck disappear and my gloves were so big that my thumbs no longer protruded, so I'm not sure how clear my response was. Somehow he got my point, though.

Once we were all loaded and sitting safely in the seats of the snow mobile, Tom hit the gas and we shot forward to what I imagined was the back yard of the cottage. I felt the snow mobile turn a corner, looked up, and saw movement of some unidentifiable shapes. It was still very difficult to see anything in the snow storm except fuzzy outlines.

"These are our dogs," Tom said with a wave of what I assumed was his hand. "We separate them into 8 cages with 4 dogs in each section." The dogs started barking. "They're Siberian Huskies and they live out here all winter."

"When do they come inside to get warm?" I shout-asked to the back of Tom's head. Seeing them curled up in the snow made me more concerned about the comfort of the dogs than I was the thrill of the sledding.

"They're used to the cold," the back of Tom's head shouted back at me. "Their fur is made so they can live in cold temperatures like today." He turned to look at me with meaningful eyes. "The thermometer said -16° when we left the cottage."

When he spoke his eyes grew wide before returning to normal size. I don't know why he chose to tell me the temperature at that time – it just made me more sad.

Our snow mobile sat in front of the cages for 10 more seconds before Tom cranked the engine again and backed away. I felt the snow mobile turn in the opposite direction toward what I assumed was a field. The longer we were out in the storm, the more difficult the world was to discern; I had to make assumptions to fill in where my vision left off.

We rode for another minute before coming to another complete stop. I saw the blur of Tom jumping off his seat in front of me and yell something to Dad I couldn't hear. Dad shouted back and they had a short conversation about what I assumed was logistics of getting on the sled. I sat and shivered until Dad's outline stood over me and reached for my legs. He was moving quickly and without consent.

"You and I are going first," he shouted. Even though his face was inches away from mine, his voice was muffled and his image was blurred.

"Go get in the sled and help me put Kristin in there," he turned and shouted to Mom.

Mom jumped off the seat behind and stepped into the frame of the metal sled Tom laid behind Dad's feet. Before I could process, Dad put his left arm under my thighs and his right arm around my waist, lifted my body off the snow mobile, and carefully plopped it in the seat. We looked at each other with wild, excited smiles.

"We're going first," Dad bent down to my ear and repeated. "Mom is going in the snow mobile with Tom and they're riding beside us with the dogs."

He pointed a blurry finger to a group of dark shadows in the otherwise complete whiteness.

I stared at the shadows and fuzzy outline of Tom and Mom in the snow mobile 100 yards in front of us. I could only barely discern Mom's dark shadow in the back seat moving a black stick next to her head. I assumed it was her hand waving, waving to no one.

"Do you know how to strap in," Tom appeared and shouted to Dad.

"Yes," Dad yelled back. He climbed into the metal seat next to me and clicked a seatbelt around his waist.

"Okay," Tom shouted. "Have fun."

He turned and did a crazy looking run-sprint to join Mom on the snow mobile.

"Here's a blanket for your legs," Dad yelled from next to me.

Yelling really wasn't necessary because we were sitting so close, but I didn't use my energy to tell him; my shivers were claiming all of my energy and I had to prioritize. He spread a wool blanket over my lap to keep my lower body warm and the snow out. I can't feel cold temperature in my legs yet, but a blanket was probably a good idea. I pictured Tammy's face pulling close to mine and shouting "just because you can't feel them doesn't mean they're not there, Kristin." I could almost feel her spit on my cheek.

I saw the blurry outline of Tom in the snow mobile facing us and holding a dark stick in the air. He was either waving or giving a thumbs up – I'm unsure exactly which one. I stuck my dark stick in the air as universal response and he whipped his body back around to face the dogs and white.

"MUSH," I barely heard Tom yell.

One dog quietly barked and our sled jerked forward. Despite the fresh, unpacked terrain, our sled slid smoothly across the ground. We jerked again and started moving at a slow but increasing pace.

"Gtsqzkdopmd," Dad screamed.

I couldn't hear him very well and couldn't make out any words, but he was probably saying something like "this is fun!" or "snow is cold!" I screamed back "yes" and shook my head up and down.

I looked around and all I could see was white. I could see the outline of Dad sitting 6 inches to my right, but I was not able to make out anything else. I could hear the smothered sound of dogs in front of us and the man on the sleigh giving commands, but those sounds were far away and hard to process. The snow was coming down so hard and so cold that all of my senses were deadened. The only thing I could focus on was keeping my fingers warm and holding on tight. True, I did lose some range of motion when I put on two winter jackets, a hoodie sweatshirt, and a neck warmer, but the world that I could see was completely whited out.

The dogs pulled me and Dad through and around the field for thirty minutes that seemed like an hour. Despite the conditions of the weather and my body temperature, I was having fun. Tom slowed down the snow mobile and our sled glided toward him and Mom, a signal for conclusion of our ride. I imagined my fingers underneath my marshmallow gloves were turning gray about to fall off and the hair on my arms stiff from the freeze. I was having a ton of fun, but I wasn't heartbroken when our ride was over.

"Whoa," I heard Tom shout when the dogs dragged us into the runway in front of the cottage.

The dogs obediently slowed down to a stop and stood in the snow, waiting for their next direction. I could make out Tom's body jumping off his seat on the sleigh to start untying ropes. The world is clearer when you're sitting still in a snow storm, as opposed to traveling at 30mph with a snowstorm assaulting your eyeballs.

"Go inside and get warm," he shouted to Dad.

I turned my head and saw all of their 3 bodies stand up and brush snow off their pants. Dad crouched to my level and Mom walked toward the cottage door with her arms full of blankets. Same as getting in the sled, Dad's hands slid under my thighs and around my waist for a lift into my waiting wheelchair.

"Did you have fun," the deep voice thundered when we shuffled through the warm-blasted cottage doors.

"It was a lot of fun," Mom spoke up.

I had a lot of fun too and wanted to report to him, but my face felt stiff and mouth was too cold to speak words.

I was still sitting in the doorway, shaking. As much of my arm as I could fit was crammed underneath my thighs and my head was hunched toward the ground. My traumatic brain injury caused the right side of my body to have poor circulation, sometimes resulting in an intense pain, loss of color, and loss of sensation in my limbs and fingers during cold conditions. And this was a cold condition.

Sitting on my hands is the fastest way to warm them and make the pain stop. All of my attention goes to relieving my cold because the pain is so much that I don't have capacity for anything else. I hunch to the ground because it helps to warm my fingers faster, or so I've tricked my mind. Needless to say, I was grateful for Mom to entertain the plaid man so I could hunch and resolve in the corner.

"That was great," Dad breezed in the doorway and into the conversation.

"I had fun," Mom added. "The dogs are cute."

"Kristin did you have fun?" Dad turned to the corner and asked.

"Uhhh" was all I could manage. Thankfully he didn't spend any more time – the adrenaline in the room was too high.

"Do you guys want some hot chocolate?" Tom swooped in the cottage door and asked. "Bill will make it for everyone."

A new man, Bill, emerged from a back room and joined the conversation without skipping a beat. He looked to each of our eyes and put up one finger for each Beale that nodded their head for hot chocolate – all of us.

"Where are you guys from?" Tom asked.

"Richmond, Virginia," Dad contributed. "We're here for Breckenridge's Wounded Warrior Ski Spectacular." He raised his arm and motioned toward me. "My daughter Kristin is skiing with them."

I raised my eyes at the mention of my name. My fingers had gone from white to red: progress. I had some feeling back in my body and the pain was fading, so I rolled over toward the conversation.

"How long have you been skiing?" Tom asked, welcoming me.

"This is my second season," I reported. My energy started to return when subject of the conversation took a turn toward Kristin. "I really like it. Breckenridge is very different from our resort in Virginia because the snow is real here."

Bill, Tom, and the Beale family sat in a circle with our hot chocolate mugs and maintained a somewhat uninteresting conversation until our driver arrived thirty minutes later. Freezing in a cottage in -16° weather and in the middle of a snowstorm is reason enough to tolerate a staling conversation; the men were friendly and talking to them made the time go by faster.

"I come to get you," the door opened and the same van driver announced to the room. I was enjoying time in the cottage, but was also happy to see its end.

"Okay," Dad stood up and turned to look at Bill and Tom. "Thank you for everything. We had a lot of fun."

"That was great," I added, now warmed enough to contribute.

"I had a good time," Mom said and grabbed her coat off the rack. I think I saw her wink at Bill, but I could have easily imagined it. Dog sledding wore me out.

"Are you ready to go now?" our driver interrupted with his overly-inquisitive voice.

"Yes," Dad said. "Rhonda will you open the van door? I'll get Kristin."

As routine, I locked the brakes on my wheelchair and he swooped down to pick up my body. One arm under my thighs, one arm around my waist, the same routine. Dad carried my shaking body out the cottage door, through the snow, and into the back seat of the van. Mom climbed in after me, followed closely by Dad and our driver. In the same way that we wave when we leave Mema and Papa's house, we all waved at Bill and Tom as we drove away and until they were out of sight.

The arguably reckless techniques of our driver snapped us quickly out of a dog-sledding mind and back into a hold-on-or-die mind. We whipped around corners, passed with no signal, and sped around pedestrians through the winded roads all the way back to our hotel. Again, slam on brakes to signal our arrival. Good thing I don't get car sick.

"Thanks for driving," Dad said and opened the door to stumble from the passenger seat.

"Yes," the driver responded. "Call if want go somewhere."

He handed Dad a business card with the corners torn off. With one more exaggerated head nod, he turned around, speed-walked to the driver's seat of his van, and drove off.

"Let's go inside the hotel," Mom suggested.

Dad nodded his head. Even though all we did was ride, the stress of the commute and the freeze of the air took all energy out of us.

I wordlessly agreed and rolled at their heels into the hotel. On the way to the door Dad reached his hand over the trash can and dropped the drivers' business card in. One dog sledding adventure is enough.

CHAPTER 10

Rowing

The water was dark but I could still see the clumps of hair, mold, and an unidentifiably gluey slush floating past the shore. Disgusting as it was, there were children at my all sides, flopping their arms and probably swallowing mouthfuls of the lake water. I grabbed the handle of my paddle and moved it to lean against my wheelchair tire.

"Is everyone ready to start rowing?" shouted Terri, our overly-excitable and oddly energizing instructor.

I met Terri through the Wintergreen Adaptive Ski program. She's on the board of Wintergreen Adaptive Sports and helps to organize days of skiing in the winter, rowing in the summer, and an overflow of sports in between.

"We're ready," responded a pre-teenaged boy sitting in a wheelchair to my right. He had either done this 100 times and lost concern for the disease-ridden water, or was a complete noob and hadn't yet considered bacterial risks of the water. Either way, he was too eager.

"Okay," said Terri with a smile covering her whole face. "Let's load into our kayaks."

I looked at the water and saw 4 able-bodied men dragging 5 kayaks, one for each disabled rower. They looked like normal kayaks except for an unmistakably higher backrest and deeper frame.

"I'll help load you in," a man came from behind me and said. "Is that okay? How do you want to do this?"

Another man walked to us and stood silently next to the first man. I think he was waiting there to help us, but I can't be certain. Maybe he was just observing.

"I'm not sure," I looked at them and said. "I don't know."

I turned to see my disabled peers loading into their kayaks with a well-practiced routine. It seemed like everyone except the three of us figured it out. And it was simple: the disabled body was being air-lifted out of the wheelchair and positioned in a kayak seat by 1 or 2 able-bodied men. It was obviously the fastest and easiest solution, but I didn't want to be the one to suggest a favor that big. Instead, I was going to make them "think of it on their own."

With all the drama I could manage, I turned my head toward the lifters and made an unnecessarily loud "hmm" noise.

"How would you feel about us picking you up and putting you in the kayak?" the first man asked. He looked at the group next to us, to me, to the second man, and back to me again. "Like they're doing."

"I guess that would be okay," I said in a fakely-hesitant voice. I wanted to make it seem like the idea of people carrying me around like royalty didn't occur to me first. I don't love the idea, but sometimes it just works better. Even still, I have to at least pretend like I have reservations.

"Okay," the second man finally spoke. "Let's do this."

The two men narrowed in on me, one on each side, and squatted down to grab my lanky body. Each man put one arm under my thigh and one arm under my armpit, then glided my body neatly onto the seat of my kayak.

"Thank you both," I said and continued to wiggle my hips into position on the kayak's seat. By the time those words were out of my mouth, the men were climbing out of the water and back up the hill. They were probably fleeing from the lump of hair-slime that I watched move through the water like it had a mind of its own. I understood.

"Everyone grab your paddles," Terri called from a kayak nearby.

I could tell by the smile in her voice that she was genuinely happy to be there. She saw me looking, of course, and gave me a seemingly exaggerated but probably sincere smile. Again, covering her whole face.

I reached for my paddle and remembered it was rested against my wheelchair on the shore. I put it there before I got into my kayak, but lost track of it after that. With a stroke of urgency, I looked around and saw it leaning horizontally in front of me on the neck of the kayak. I looked up further and saw the first man floating past me in front. He winked and nodded his head as if to say "I did that. You're welcome."

"Then move your body like this," I heard the end of Terri's sentence to the group of floating rowers. I tuned back in and saw her leaning her body weight towards the water to her right, while keeping her left paddle in the water.

"What is she doing?" I whispered to myself. It appeared to be a basic skill of paddling in a kayak, but I was [over-]confident that I didn't need instruction on something so simple. I'm not sure where that confidence was coming from.

"Okay," Terri shouted to us. "You guys have fun."

Like dogs out of a garage, my fellow disabled athletes had their paddles in hand and raced toward the middle of the lake as soon as she gave word. I, on the other hand, didn't listen to the instructions and fumbled with my paddle. I couldn't even get my boat moving.

I didn't want anyone to see my struggle, though, because I didn't want to sit through more instruction and wasting more time. So, I slunk my body down and found an alternative: while no one was looking, I stuck my paddle through the water, dug it into the muddy ground, and pushed off.

I spent the next hour and a half anchoring my paddle in the mud, rowing in circles, and avoiding further instruction by keeping a happy and laidback expression on my face. I did my best to float either in the shallow water so my paddle could reach the bottom, or close to objects so I could push off.

Quickly and understandably that got boring and a little bit lonely. I couldn't keep up with the other rowers in the middle of the lake, so I hung on the sidelines and spun in circles while everyone else played Tag and Mother May I.

"Okay everyone," Terri's voice yelled after what seemed like 2 hours of spinning in circles. "It's time to come in."

Her words were followed by a chorus of moans from my peers. In my head, I was singing and cheering with joy.

Terri and her group of disabled ducklings turned their kayaks and started moving toward the edge of the lake with ease and control. There was a crowd of parents standing on the land and I saw Mom waving at me energetically. I was planning on telling her I had fun kayaking. I was not planning on telling her that her 17 year old daughter just spent the last 2 hours just trying to paddle the kayak.

I did a combination of pushing off the ground and spinning in half-circles until I reached the shore. I had a little bit of a head start because I had stayed so close to the edge the whole time, so my kayak and I were able to arrive at the same time as everyone else. Honestly, I don't think they even realized I was missing from the group. That was my first victory.

My second victory was managing to stay out of the water the whole time; the only part of my body that got the slime on it was my fingertips from holding the wet handle of the paddle. My dry-body-win was thanks to the two men who followed me around like it was their job, doing my dirty work of transferring my body in and out of the water and muck.

"Did you have fun?" Mom speed-walked toward me and asked almost as soon as I got within earshot of the shore. She was holding a towel to rub on my dry skin.

"I had fun," I responded energetically. It wasn't a lie. I had fun before and after I was in the kayak – she never specified a time.

"That was great," Terri beamed from behind us. "Everyone had so much fun."

That she believed "everyone had fun" means I was successful in hiding my lack of enjoyment and complete lack of skill. Bravo, Kristin.

"Yes we did," shouted the overzealous kid from before. "I'll be back next month. I can't wait."

Mom looked down at me with a pleasant smile on her face.

"Do you want to do this again next month?" she asked, so naïve.

"Maybe," I said. "It depends on some things." She grabbed the towel from me and we headed back up the ramp toward the car.

It depended on nothing. One afternoon of rowing is enough for me for the rest of my life. Luckily, she never asked about it again.

CHAPTER 11

Children's Hospital Outpatient

Mom and I pulled into the parking lot of the Children's Hospital Outpatient building and I crammed the rest of a turkey sandwich in my mouth. We were running late and my window to work out before going back to school was getting smaller with every mouthful of lunch. Knowing that, I was taking as many mouthfuls as I could.

Three school days per week, I forfeited lunchtime with my friends at high school to go to Children's Hospital Outpatient. In the hour-long lunch window, I practiced walking with a walker and parallel bars. I got to get away from my school building for a mid-day brace-walk to practice my gait, in anticipation of walking across the stage to receive my diploma at my high school graduation. It was nice to get away, yes, but I can think of 100 other things I would rather do with my escape.

A one hour workout to break up the school day sounds like a great idea on paper, right? But the reality is, that place was a drag. The gym is small, therapists were slimy, and I was surrounded by people who didn't believe in my full rehabilitation. My therapist, Tina, was the only exception.

When we opened the door to the gym, Mom and I went immediately to the back room. With my bag of leg braces in her arms, she ran ahead to sit on a blue mat and motioned my wheelchair in front. As routine, I pulled up and she grabbed my foot from its footplate to take off my Converse shoe. I unloaded my leg brace, unstrapped the Velcro, and slid my leg into the plastic, hip-high frame.

I don't like to brag, but Mom and I could fully brace my legs in under 2 minutes time – 7 minutes faster than any other mom/child team. Maybe I am bragging a little bit.

Tina also had her timing down. She somehow always skipped out of her office door in the same minute of us finishing.

"Are you ready to get started?" she asked in a disgustingly insouciant voice from across the unreasonably compact workout area. I nodded and she continued a strut toward an equipment closet to get my loaner walker.

"How are you?" Mom half-shouted to the back of Tina head.

"I'm okay," Tina shouted back. "Busy. A lot of new kids coming in this week."

She reappeared from the closet and started walking toward us with a gray, rusted walker in her hand. The gym is only about 15 steps wide, so she stood in front us in about 2 seconds – too soon in my opinion.

She slammed the walker on the floor in front of me and stepped back with an expecting look on her face.

"Oh," I moaned.

It wasn't a surprised "oh!" – just crestfallen. No matter how many times I practice and until I become an expert, brace-walking will always dishearten me.

Tina nudged the leg of the walker with her toe either in attempt to motivate me or command me – it was probably a little of both. I truly didn't want to understand her nonverbal orders, but they were hard to ignore. Plus, now she had Mom's attention.

"C'mon sweetie," Mom hummed from my diagonal. "Let's get walking."

With zero enthusiasm, I grabbed the handles and wobbled the frame back and forth until the legs were aligned. I inched my own legs in front of me and scooted my butt to the edge of the mat.

"I'll ground it," Tina blurted and held tight to the handles to push into the carpet. This time I could ignore her because she says and does the same thing every time I stand – there's no need to confirm.

I reached out and grabbed the washcloth-padded handles of the walker and pulled it close to my body. Next, I bent my elbows at 90° and pushed myself up until I was at 45°, an almost-standing position. From there, I redirect and push my body vertically so my legs will fall into place under me. Once I'm standing I use my arms to wiggle my body around in circles until my hips face forward and I'm at a comfortable posture. I flex each of my wrists and graze my hands over my washcloths.

When that first routine is complete, I put myself through a second routine that is very precise and purposely time consuming. First I adjust my feet to face forward and pull my shirt down. I push my watch up my arm to avoid interference with the bend of my wrist, then I move my bracelet up my opposite arm in the same manner. I will pull down my shirt again and run my hand through my hair to get it out of my eyes before rechecking my feet to make sure they're next to each other with toes in front. Throughout these routines I maintain an air of importance, pushing Mom and Tina to wait and watch without asking questions. I have long lost track of whether my routines are out of necessity or a giant stall tactic but, either way, routine is routine. Respect tradition.

"Okay Kristin," Mom said after 3 minutes of waiting for me to finish. My personal victory is when I can get a full 3 minutes out of it. "Time to walk."

From the corner of my eye I saw Tina nod her head and a stream of annoyance ran through me. Lifting my eyes past her and up only slightly, I looked to the hallway I was walking through: my runway.

"Get it over with," I thought to myself and pushed the walker forward a few inches. I pushed my body off the ground so it was suspended in the air, and grounded it four inches forward. At that point it was more of a hop than a step. I made my first hop out of what felt like one trillion.

By the time I made my ninth step I was only at the blue mat in the middle of the small gym. Tina slithered behind me and strapped a "safety-gait-belt" so tightly around my abdomen that it rode up my torso and dug into my ribs. Despite my discomfort, I stayed quiet and chose not to fight the freedom-from-gait-belt-battle again. I also didn't want to interrupt Tina and Mom's conversation because I was avoiding dialogue as much as possible. They were talking about our trip to California and I had long ago blocked them out.

I walked down the long, colorless hall and counted every step I took. The more I stepped, the closer and more tunneled my vision was to my finish line: a blue chair at the end of the hall. I concentrated on that chair and walked with a purpose.

"Yeah," I heard Mom bragging from behind me. "It was pretty intense. We had a four to six hour workout every day."

I tuned into their conversation. By "we had a four to six hour workout," she really meant "I sat in the waiting room and read a book for four to six hours while Kristin worked out." It made her feel good to say "we" and I didn't have the energy to crush her esteem. She is so cute.

When I finally arrived at the bathroom at the middle of the hallway, it seemed like I had been walking for one week. The waiting room was close in my vision, but still a far reach of my walking. My palms were aching red and shoulders throbbing.

"Just a little further," Tina announced.

I gave her a weak grunt of recognition and moved the walker forward. My body was fatiguing and it showed in my next step: I lifted my legs off the ground, lost some control, and plopped my legs down with a thud. My movements were getting lazier, but that didn't bother me as much as it should have. My eyes were fixed on the end of the hallway.

At long last, I reached the blue chair. Now, my last responsibility is to sit down politely. It sounds easy, but this is usually the most difficult part – relaxation is so close and precision is so hard with an entirely fatigued body. It also requires a lot of balance and stability that I lack.

"Okay Kristin," Tina said from behind me. "Remember our practice."

I nodded my head once then lifted the walker up to put it down one inch to the left of my foot. I unweighted both of my legs, dropped them 2 more inches to my right, and regained my balance. I repeated that process eight more times before the blue chair was diagonal to my body.

Without fail and every time I move from standing to sitting in my leg braces, I run out of patience and disregard all technique I've endlessly practiced. I let my body fall back into the chair, only partially in control.

Also without fail, Tina scampers to my side and quiet-screams a lot of words, none that I could process. She splattered my face with spit but, still, I wasn't paying much attention. At that point I was far past the point of caring how graceful I look during my unload. My mind was focused on relaxing in that chair and nothing was going to get in my way.

As soon as I sat down, though, Tina attacked. It was like she had been holding it in the whole time.

"When you sit down," she started, "you really need to watch where you're sitting and feel behind you. You also need to…"

I didn't hear the rest. I did, however, feel several drops of warm saliva land on my cheek.

"You have one minute of break left," she announced after she had settled down.

I made a tired sort of "ehh" noise and looked at her staring at her wrist watch. Tina started timing my breaks because she figured out my trick: when my time was almost up I started a conversation about something I knew she liked. This almost always made her start talking about it, get distracted, more of my time wasted, less time for me to walk. It was a well-practiced and highly successful plan. But now she figured me out and timed them. No more tricks.

"Okay," she said and slammed the walker in front of me again. She waived her hand toward it. "Your rest is over."

As habit, I grabbed the handles, lifted my body off the ground, and went through an abbreviated version of my standing routine. Because we were in the bottom of the hour, the speed of my walking directly affected how soon I could plant myself in my wheelchair and roll out.

"Okay," I said through heavy breaths. "Here we go." I gave Mom a meaningful look, but not too meaningful. I wanted her distracted so she could keep Tina distracted.

I fought through five minutes of uninterrupted anticipation on my walk back to the gym. The visual of my chair parked next to the mat made it pass a ton easier and a little bit quicker, but still I felt every second.

I repeated the same falling motion into my chair and, no surprise, listened to Tina give the same lecture. It was more bearable this time, though, because my mind was focused on tearing the Velcro and untying my leg straps as fast as possible. Mom joined me and we undressed my legs in record time.

"Bye," I mumbled to Tina, almost without pause from cramming my braces into their bag. I didn't look her in the eyes.

Mom, on the other hand, paused thoughtfully and turned around to face her.

"What did you say was the name of the island you went to?" she asked.

I dropped my head down in a muted and over exaggerated reaction to her chattiness. My head-drop combined with taking my brace-bag from her hand came across clearly. She got my hint and wrapped it up.

"I'll see you tomorrow," Tina said and turned to walk back to her office, also without pause. She must have known an after-workout conversation wouldn't last long. She knew I had tunnel vision.

I give the same "uhhh" noise for every therapist I had in the first years of my disability. It's not because they weren't great to me and necessary in making me the independent adult woman I eventually became, but their timing was just bad. My memory of those therapists is lame because, at the time, everything associated with my disability was lame. I had trouble switching from a "learn to walk" mindset to a "sit in a wheelchair" mindset, and they all seemed to be pushing for the latter. It was tricky. I tried to keep my eyes focused on walking as much as I could and, as consequence, the people trying to improve my wheelchair-circumstance were understandably agitating. It took a while for me to reach a balance. Most of them were good in some way, though. Tina was one of the good ones.

"Okay," I responded. Now I was talking to Tina as she walked away. How the tables turn.

"You did well today," Mom looked down to me and sang.

"Thank you," I mumbled, then turned to roll through the hallway and into the warm outside air.

I arrived at Mom's car, loaded my braces into the trunk, and transferred into the passenger seat in one motion. My back and shoulders were drawn up and sore from pushing on the walker and my palms were red with anger.

Like many things in my life post-accident, it's extremely humbling to have to work as hard as I did and as hard as I could to make one short walk down a hallway. It's interesting to think about how little effort and how quickly this walk would take me before my accident, as opposed to how large of an effort and how much time it takes me now. Those are the kind of things you don't realize until it's too late, though – only after they're taken away.

The next step in my progress is crutches; when arm crutches are in the picture, things get serious. They're probably the most difficult form of adaptive walking and, no surprise, my next goal. As soon as I mastered a walker, I planned on throwing those skills out the window and moving up. Crutches are a giant move up. Challenge accepted.

Mom climbed into the seat next to me without a word, started the car, and started the drive back to school. I closed my eyes and relaxed against the seat, hoping to catch a few minutes of homeroom before Chemistry class. The only thing worse than brace walking, I've found, is Chemistry class.

CHAPTER 12

Lacrosse

O n Friday, Kristin got some of the best news she's had in some time. She was officially asked to be the Assistant Coach for the Wildcats Girls Lacrosse team. Many of you may remember that Rhonda and Kristin started the team last year because of Kristin's interest in the game. They had an outstanding response to the initial formation and even had enough to have 2 teams. Kristin loved playing lacrosse. Again, this year there has been a large contingency.

Rhonda took her to her first practice on Saturday with some anxiety and sorrow in her heart. It was good to see her so excited, but sad because all she could see were images in the past of Kristin running on the field. It's a complicated emotion to be happy and sad for someone at the very same time; you don't know whether to smile or cry. In either case, the result is the same...it moves you to cry. As she fought those tears, Kristin said, "You know, Mom, things are really starting to come around now; I feel like my life is coming together." As Kristin wheeled out to the field, it became even harder for Rhonda, but down deep, it was good to hear her optimism.

When I went to pick her up, I witnessed a Living Moment from those girls on the team. Kristin met me half way on the field. It was the end of practice and the coach came up and said, "Kristin, blow the whistle and get them over here; it's time for sprints." Kristin blew the whistle and held her hands out as if preparing to hug someone. They all came over without hesitation as if bees to honey. They stood in front of her and then I saw and heard it...

*"1...2...3...**BEALE!**"*

I had heard that the girls always did that before every game as a tribute to Kristin, but to see it brought a whole new perspective. I looked at Kristin and it really brings a smile on her face. Sometimes, I feel like we're waiting, waiting, waiting...for something "big" to happen with her physically. I've learned that anything, big or small, that brings even a minute of happiness to her, is BIG. This coaching position is very big for her and she is looking forward to it with great excitement.

"Ball, ball, ball," I screamed and pushed my wheelchair to the corner of the gymnasium.

Everybody heard my voice but nobody looked at me. The ball was literally never passed to me. I was the only girl in a gym full of teenaged boys, so nothing I did or said held any credibility.

It was day two of a two-day-long adaptive lacrosse clinic. Two wheelchair-bound men, one who was especially attractive, were flown from Southern California to a school in the middle of Nowhere, Virginia to teach the sport to 15-20 disabled teenagers, myself included. I heard about the clinic and jumped on the opportunity, any opportunity, to learn a new adaptive sport – especially lacrosse.

Lacrosse was a significant part of my able-bodied time in grade school. I loved, excelled in, and depended on it during the four months of spring semester. Ever since I was a child, sports have played an important role in my life. When I was younger, I was involved in soccer, gymnastics, and cheerleading. As I grew into my teenage years, soccer and gymnastics were replaced by field hockey and lacrosse, and sideline cheerleading turned into competition cheerleading. Athletics were a way for me to let out my childhood energy and later teenage angst.

But lacrosse was my favorite of them all. My favor ran so deep that Mom and I had the idea for, established, and managed a lacrosse program at my high school. During my freshman year, I earned the title of captain of a team of my peers. It's unclear whether I was captain because I'm the daughter of the founder of the team or because I was an exceptional player, but I prefer the latter and am uninterested in the truth.

"Everyone form a group in the middle of the floor," the attractive coach shouted and pointed his finger toward the basketball court. "We're going to scrimmage."

The group of boys around me burst into a choir of cheers and excitement. I, on the other hand, filled with dread. I tried so hard to enjoy lacrosse in its adaptive form, but it disheartened me a little bit. Before my accident, lacrosse meant so much to me; I worked hard and was very good at it.

Lacrosse in the adaptive version, though, required me to learn new skills I struggled with: balancing a lacrosse stick and ball in my lap while I wheel around the court; keeping my balance while I knock other people's stick; playing with deeper pockets and no safety zone; and so much more I never learned as a teenager and had trouble succeeding in. Honestly, I was frustrated with adaptive lacrosse because it didn't come to me naturally. Because I had already worked to become proficient with my able body, it was frustrating to start over with my disabled body.

Another thing to consider is my lack of practice. All the other boys at the clinic were either preexisting friends or shared an immediate male bond that I was excluded from. Because of that, they only communicated with and passed the ball to each other and ignored me, the overzealous, weird-looking girl who kept yelling for the ball from the corner of the gym. That resulted in my inability to practice, learn the sport, improve, and have fun. In the rare instances somebody actually passed the ball to me, I got so excited that I would fumble around and eventually drop it, making myself an even less appealing team member. I can't be but so mad at them.

"Matthew and Sean can be team captains," the attractive coach said. He raised his finger and pointed to the two loudest, most obnoxious boys in the group. "Go to the middle of the gym and pick your team members."

Matthew and Sean looked at each other with fake competitiveness and wheeled to the front of the group. They started rolling through names and, within minutes, two groups of wheelchairs formed in the middle of the court. I sat and listened to everybody's names being called except for myself and a nerdy-looking boy sitting to the left of me. All around me were memories of the boys already assigned to a team and I expected the worst: I will be chosen last.

Sitting proudly in front of two large groups of wheelchair-bound boys, I watched the captains look to me, the nerd, and then each other with expressions that said "it doesn't matter which person we choose – they're both incapable."

"I'll take Sam," Matthew shouted through squinted eyes.

The nerdy-looking kid sitting next to me smiled, bounced in his chair, and pushed himself to the group of boys on the left of the gym.

"Okay Sean," the attractive coach said. "Kristin is on your team."

Sean gave the coach an obedient smile and spun his chair around without looking me in the eyes. I was an outcast.

The scrimmage started, the boys laughed and howled, and I slunk into the sidelines. The less attractive coach acted as referee and engaged with the boys playing in the scrimmage, and the attractive coach parked his chair next to the equipment to watch. I recognized an opportunity and rolled to him.

"Which part of California are you from?" I asked in my sweetest voice.

"We're both from Los Angeles," he turned his chair to face me and smiled.

"I went to Los Angeles one time to try adaptive surfing," I said, trying to find a common ground. "I saw a little bit of the area, but mostly just Newport Beach."

"Oh really," he said with a flattering upward inflection. I appreciated him pretending to be interested in my life. "Are you from California?"

"No," I said with a new burst of energy. "I've visited there a lot to work out in Solana Beach, though."

During the next 20 minutes of the scrimmage [that I thankfully wasn't a part of], our conversation extended into sharing accident stories, me telling him about Awakenings, conversation about living in LA, and any other intimate fact about myself I could connect to the context of the conversation. It didn't take long for us to figure out that Laura, the founder and owner of Awakenings, is a mutual friend. I sat on the sideline and had a detail-specific conversation with the attractive coach instead of playing in the scrimmage. I was happy.

"Okay guys," the less attractive coach yelled. "Our time is up. Let's bring it in."

In unison, a disappointed moan leaked from all the boys' mouths. In my head, I rejoiced.

"Today was great," he said to the group of boys that formed around him. "You've all improved so much since yesterday."

That didn't include me, obviously.

As the less attractive coach said final words to the group of boys, the gym started to fill with parents coming to pick up their sons. By that point I wasn't paying any attention to what he was saying. I turned and saw Mom and Dad smiling beside the door leading to the outside of the gym.

The attractive coach rolled away from the group and started conversation with a parent before I could get to him, so I sat at a patient distance behind so I could steal his next free moment to engage. I wasn't going to let him get away again. I was like a tiger.

"It was nice to meet you," I blurted as soon as he finished his conversation and the mother turned to leave.

"Yes definitely," he turned to me and said with an appealing smile. "Maybe I'll see you around some time."

"I hope so," I said. These are the moments I wish I knew how to wink. "Thank you for everything today."

I gave him a smile that felt cute. I don't know how it looked, but it felt cute.

He smiled back at me and his face was flawless. That's probably the last time I'll see him, but it felt okay. I spun my chair, chucked my borrowed stick in the equipment pile, and rolled to my parents standing at the door. I was trying for a dramatic exit.

Adaptive lacrosse is a sport I don't think I'll ever play again. It was dispiriting to have to relearn what I had already worked so hard and become so good at years before. When I had my accident, I was an experienced player with an athletic body and a cute butt. Really, I would rather just end my lacrosse memories with that.

CHAPTER 13

Crutch Walking

"I just need a second," I breathed. My voice came out as a whisper. "My head feels like it's floating away from my body."

I lifted my head up one more inch to look at the end of the blue tape that lined my runway. My arms and shoulders were fatigued as response to my vacation the week before, and my head felt weirdly isolated. I was not a happy camper.

"Come on," blurted my therapist, Tina, with an energy that didn't match the early morning. "Let's keep it going."

Her voice squeaked in my ear and sent a tingle down my spine. I forced a small smile and nodded my head one time with acknowledgement. I was practicing patience.

Earlier that month when Tina went on vacation, I walked with a different therapist and very quickly realized that she's the only person who can get me to work – everyone else is just too easy to trick. She learned my stalling tactics and didn't fall for any of them anymore: scratching my nose for extra seconds, start conversation I knew she would engage in, and/or talk to the people around me so she'll feel rude to interrupt. I hadn't had luck with those for a while, but now she knew them all and I had to work.

I moved my crutch in front of me then positioned my legs, hips, and crutches for the next step. My biceps felt like they were coming out of my skin.

> *Amazed...*
>
> *...at what the human spirit can accomplish. Kristin has been training on crutches. She attaches braces on her legs from her feet to her hips. She started with a walker and braces. Moving 2 legs at once in short "swings" in the walker, she went from just managing to stand up, to using the walker to move 20 or more feet. Using the walker was very hard on her hands and upper body, as all of her weight would bear down on the walker. When she felt like she had "mastered" the walker, she wanted to start on crutches. This is much more difficult because they are not in a fixed position. Still, she hasn't used a walker in about 3-4 months because she was so focused on the crutches. Again, her goal is to walk across the stage to receive her diploma. My little girl isn't going to give up.*

"Last week it helped to line up your crutch with this leg," Mom said from behind me. She stepped forward and pointed to the ground next to my right. "Remember?"

"I don't remember," I whispered. I placed the crutch ahead of me and took more steps. More steps, I guess, until I either fall down or my hour is up.

It seems like every time I walk with crutches I discover and lean on a new method to get me through the therapy hour. As soon as they end, all those hours clump into one big section of my life titled "No Smiles." I keep coming back, though, because the torture I endured with crutch walking is the torture that'll make me stronger and put me closer to my goal of walking across the stage at my high school graduation. That made me feel better, but only a tiny bit.

Walking with crutches is different from walking with a walker which, I thought I would never say, is a comfort zone for me. With a walker all I have to do is slam the frame in front and step forward; it's anchored together so I don't have to worry about where to position my legs in relation to the walker's leg. I worked at perfecting my walker-walking every morning for an entire summer and months into the school year, so it was a huge victory when I was finally comfortable with it. As soon as that happened, though, I moved up to the next hardest thing: crutches. The fun never stops. I can never stop.

Almost no skills I mastered while walking with a walker translate into skills I need for walking with crutches, either. It is a whole new world. "Fun" is a terrible word to use.

Before I take each step with a crutch, the crutch corresponding with the stepping-leg needs to be behind me so I can shift all my weight to my other side to un-weight my moving-leg. The other crutch has to be in front and about three inches to the side of my standing leg. If it's too close and I try to un-weight, I'll fall over the crutch, hit my head on the ground, and die. Again, very dramatic.

"Good stepping," Tina shouted, always too suddenly. "You're getting the hang of it now."

I'm not sure what I was doing right. I'm never exactly sure what I'm doing when I walk with crutches. Something was working, though, so I kept stepping.

Thirty cruel minutes of my unreasonably slow walking pace passed and I finally reached the halfway point of the gym – another three feet to go. Mom and Tina were talking about the weather and I blocked them out. My crutch walking was still in its early stages, extra slow, and requires my full concentration; it takes me 5 minutes and all of my focus to walk twelve measly inches. My shoulders, biceps, and triceps burn and my upper body feels like it will combust at any moment.

In those moments of suffering, my mind is only capable of producing negative thoughts: Sheila, my personal trainer, is on vacation in the Bahamas; the gait belt around my stomach is too small and too tight; I cut my hair too short and it keeps getting stuck in my mouth; and my entire body throbs. Sometimes it makes me feel better to whine about things – if only in my own head.

"Come on sweetie," Mom chimed. "You can do this. Let's go."

I realized the furrowed brow and slanted mouth my face was making. Like always, Mom was tuned in to my frustration and took on Sheila's role of replacement cheerleader to get me through the Crutch Walking Hell I was in. Her efforts were weak, but so was my body.

I repositioned my crutch then stumbled and hopped the remaining gap to the blue tape. As quickly as Tina could retrieve and position my wheelchair behind me, I twisted my hips and fell back into my wheelchair's cushion. Once again and like always, ignoring all skills I learned for a graceful descent.

Relaxing into my seat brought me relative happiness. I was still under the beading eyes of Tina, but I was also finally able to unclench my shoulders and try to tune out my surroundings for my one minute of rest.

"Your break is over," Tina's unpleasant voice sang after 60 too-short seconds passed. It felt like half that time. "Time to walk."

I looked at the clock with only 15 minutes to go. Fifteen minutes left of torture then I was out the door with a three day workout-weekend of me. Factor in 5 minutes to take off my braces and 5 minutes of stalling, and I only had 5 more minutes to crutch walk. I rolled to the beginning of the tape and brought my arms back into a 90° angle.

Tina and Mom picked back up on their uninteresting conversation and I went back into my head – surviving the rest of the journey back to the gym and through the door was the only thing on my mind. With motivation of the weekend, I put the crutch in front of me, moved my leg forward, and took a step. One down, 300 to go.

Friday, June 6 (2 years & 10 months after injury)
– An entry from Dad's CaringBridge journal.

"Ain't God great?!" So aptly put by Kristin so many years ago as she skipped down the halls of our church; life was good, she knew why it was good and she didn't mind letting everyone know it.

Last night, she proclaimed the same message, but showed it instead of verbalizing it. On the same floor that, she had competed in a cheering competition a few short years ago, she was now going to show a large venue full of people of all ages that the human spirit is a mighty force. Kristin is going to walk across the stage to receive her high school diploma.

"...and whatever you do, don't fall, little girl" were my final words before we left the house.

"Don't worry, Dad. I GOT this."

We left the house after a short gathering of guests, which included both sets of grandparents and friends. There were about 24 of us. We were making sure a cheering squad was on hand, but we later found that was not necessary.

Kristin was beautiful. Her face was lit up; she was so happy in anticipation of what was to come. We were able to get decent seats to tape the entire event. Kristin had her leg braces on, along with her favorite Nike shoes. She was ready to go.

After 2 ceremony-practice runs earlier this week, the Deep Run staff had everything set up perfectly. The walker was on the stage. I holding it together pretty well until I saw her position herself on stage in front of the walker. The most challenging part of the brace-walking process is going from the chair to a standing position because your knees are locked. Imagine having to use all upper body strength to press down on the walker's handles to lift your body, while simultaneously moving your body forward. With no lower abdominal muscles. For Kristin, it went without a hitch. I couldn't see a hint of struggle beyond the smile that covered her face. She has been working so hard for this.

"Kristin Elizabeth Beale."

As her name was called, she rose from her wheelchair and took her first steps. The clapping began and continually escalated as she steadily moved across the stage. After about 4 steps, the entire Siegel Center rose to a standing ovation. Over 5,000 people clapping and cheering until she made it all the way across. It took about 30 seconds, but I could have watched for hours. Her face was beaming.

She's been interviewed a couple of times recently. The basic message is clear although not articulated in this manner...faith in God, faith in herself, and the support of believers in what she's trying to do will allow her to accomplish whatever she wants to do. She's gone from a "complete" injury to "incomplete", to moving her toes, to moving her legs and, finally, to reciprocating brace-walking. There's more to come.

"Well, you did it. You managed to get 5,000 people to stand up and cheer you on. Pretty impressive."

"People stood up? I didn't notice."

I laughed, "Kristin, how could you not notice?"

"I was so focused on walking across the stage. I had tunnel vision."

The most moving part of this experience was to see everyone come to their feet in honor of Kristin. It did the heart good to see the support. I have mentioned in earlier posts about those that are critical or make derogatory comments about our situation. The majority of the time, things you say about people will eventually get back to the person; it's true. But those things get vaporized when you see so much positive like last night. So much love and support; truly incredible.

Ain't God great?!

CHAPTER 14

Awakenings

We've come to the realization that the best results in Kristin's journey come from her extensive training in California. Our debate has been whether to simply take her to California for one year to do all that we can do as soon as we can do it. This means her being out of school, the family being separated and Kristin having "no life" without her friends. All of these things are important, but if we don't do it, we might look back and regret not taking the opportunity. This is to say nothing of the pure expense.

After a lot of thought and praying, we've decided to take her back for one month intervals every quarter beginning in January, tentatively. She'll *go, get a "shot in the arm," come back and work here at home, and then go back on as soon as she can. Deep Run High School has been absolutely tremendous in cooperating with us. This plan allows her to graduate with her class, be active with her friends, keep our family together and will be less of a financial drain on the family. Kristin has agreed with this plan.*

At this point, we are trying to locate a tutor for Kristin to use in California. The tutor will work with Deep Run on Kristin's assignments, tests, etc. to keep her current.

We're all determined to do everything possible to give Kristin a fighting chance. For all of her hard work, she deserves at least that.

Of all the places I've traveled and rehabilitation gyms I've visited, Awakenings Health Institute in Solana Beach, California is my favorite. Apart from the consistent and ideal weather conditions, California is a breath of fresh air for anyone looking for an untraditional approach to recovery.

I heard about Awakenings, actually, at the end of a workout at Project Walk. Sarah, a friend and fellow client, said she had "found a gym twenty minutes away" and, to my disbelief, she liked it better. At that time Project Walk was my Mecca. What could be better?

With my motto "leave no stone unturned" hanging over my head, I signed myself up for 2 hour workouts at Project Walk in the morning, and 2 more hours working out at Awakenings in the afternoon. It was a crazy time for me.

There is an energy and attitude at Awakenings that is unique to anything I've found on the East Coast; there's a fellowship in the gym that's not only inviting, but provides a sense of belonging. At home I'm pushed to accept and accommodate life in a wheelchair, where in California I have the resources and opportunity to improve my health, restore movement and sensation to my body, and ultimately better my lifestyle. The disabled community of Awakenings does an outstanding job of exceeding the preconceptions of hopelessness that doctors on the East Coast drilled into my and my family's head since day one.

The real progress that's made with Kristin has a common denominator… her trips to California. There, she's surrounded by people that believe in her potential to walk again. It's a mindset that has power beyond comprehension, at times. Momentum is a powerful tool. She grows stronger and more determined with each new development.

"We're right on time," I said as I transferred out of the car and into my wheelchair's cushion. The mornings before workouts at Awakenings seemed to take forever to get started. Probably because I was very excited to work out and counted down the minutes until I got to the gym. I realize how weird that is.

With Mom in my wake, I rolled down the concrete sidewalk and past the open windows of the business office next to me. It took a conscious effort to turn my head in the opposite direction to avert my eyes from the young men and women sitting at business desks, instead of staring them all down like I wanted to. The view I was averting to, though, was the ocean-side Design District and Pacific Ocean bordering Solana Beach, California. So it wasn't that big of a sacrifice.

"Go ahead," Mom said from behind me when we arrived at the front door. Her voice sounded distant. "I'm going for a walk on the beach. I'll see you after your workout."

I turned and saw only the back of her head speed-walking back down the sidewalk toward the parking lot. Instead of sitting on the couch at the front of the gym and reading a book for four hours a day while I'm with a trainer, Mom discovered a beach in walking distance.

Everything about that made me jealous. I so desperately want to be able to walk on the beach next to her. I imagine the feeling of the wet sand on the bottom of my feet from the waves that consumed the ground seconds before. I remember the hot sand and how I would run back and forth from hot sand to cool water until I couldn't stand it anymore. I miss playing on the beach but, most of all, how the hard ground felt on the bottoms of my feet. I didn't realize how much we sense through our feet, of course, until I lost the ability. There are times even now, more than a decade into my paralysis, I long for that feeling back just as acutely as I did when I was newly injured. Those memories never go away.

But that's why I come to California.

> *Over the past 4 months, Kristin spent 3 of those weeks in San Diego at Awakenings Health Institute in a physical therapy program. Awakenings was her decided favorite of places that give hope to spinal cord injury victims. She was pushed to extremes, which is an environment that she strives in. When she was told to "Come on! Do 2 more! You're almost there!" she would respond with, "No, I'm doing 5" or "Just 30 more seconds!" she would go an extra 30 seconds. I'll never forget when she came home from the hospital how she pulled herself up the stairs in our house and didn't stop until she was all the way to the top. It is one of a long list of how determined Kristin is in everything she does. When she sets her mind on something, she gives it everything she's got. She is our hero.*

"Good morning," I announced as I rolled into the front door. At this early hour I was the only client in the gym. All of the lights were off and Angela, who usually sits at the front desk, was in the kitchen making coffee.

"Good morning, Kristin," she shouted back at me with enthusiasm that only emphasized my own. "Laura is in the back."

I rolled forward to the stack of black mats and dragged them to the ground. I don't know which exercise I was setting up for, but there's about 70 percent chance there will be black mats involved. I was being proactive.

"Good morning, kid," Laura glided through the door and said, also with a refreshing enthusiasm.

Laura is the person who motivates me the most in the world. Her personal experience with a spinal cord injury means she can understand unique struggles in my and other clients' lives, while also maintaining an attitude of persistence that doesn't allow for excuses or give-ups. In the same way, Awakenings is like no place I've been before; working out is something I love and look forward to. I'm surrounded by acceptance and tolerance unique from anything I've felt at home or any other facility I've visited. People are just happy here.

> *She's back in California.*
> *The rehab of her body always reaches a peak out there. The positive energy that flows from her trainers is endless. They never tire nor do they seem to look at it as a "job". There is a level of sincerity that is rarely seen by anyone in her care. To be constantly working with spinal cord injury patients all day, every day, and sustain a positive attitude, takes a special person. Laura, Kristin's trainer at Awakenings Health Institute, was very taken with Kristin and observed that she has a head start on her recovery because of her positive mental attitude.*
>
> *Laura said she can tell that Kristin "really wants to walk and her attitude is going to be the biggest part of her recovery." Travis, at Project Walk, said almost the exact same thing, "There is a huge connection between mind and body in this process." Kristin understands this and it relentless in her workout schedule.*

"Good morning," I said with matching energy.

All the tired was gone from my body and replaced by eagerness. Soon after starting a workout with Laura that eagerness turns to intensity, intensity turns into determination, determination turns to fatigue. Those are the workouts that get results and those are the workouts that will teach my body to move, feel, and walk.

"We're going to start off on the Power Plate, then the Total Gym, then standing at the parallel bars," Laura said and she walked across the empty room. With apologetic eyes, I looked down at my neatly arranged black mats on the floor and rolled over them and to the Power Plate.

The Power Plate. As soon as that registered in my mind the apology left my face and was replaced first by dread, then angst. It's is my least favorite piece of equipment not because of the results that come, but because of its method of getting those results: a circular, black plate vibrates hard and fast until my brain comes loose and my body is as cold and clammy as possible. As it goes, the Power Plate is also one of the most valuable pieces of equipment because it improves circulation, lymphatic drainage, and just shakes things around to wake it up. Blah, blah, blah.

"We won't be on this for long," Laura reassured. She could either read the expression on my face, or remembered my discontent.

Her body leaped in front of mine and she started placing blocks and straps on the platform of the machine.

"You're going to kneel right here and vibrate." She pointed to the middle and most dreadful part of the Plate and looked up to smile at me. She knew what she was doing and surely she didn't expect me to smile back.

"I'll do it for you," I said with a half-smirk on my face. I knew I wasn't going to get out of it, so I might as well dedicate my session. I was half-smirking because I halfway wanted to scream and, despite my current situation, halfway wanted to hug her.

Reluctantly, I slunk out of my wheelchair onto the ground. Laura helped move my string-bean-legs from behind me and into position in front.

I kneeled in the middle of the plate and Laura pushed the "Start" button three times for three 30-second-long vibrating sessions. Thirty seconds doesn't sound like a long time when you're standing or sitting on solid ground but, on the Power Plate, those 3 sessions last 3 years.

When one and a half minutes had passed and she finally stopped pushing the button, my body slid to the ground like a slinky. The only response I knew was to lie on the floor with my hands in my armpits and mouth as straight as a line. I felt my hardened back muscles against the carpet, my shoulders were raised to touch the bottom of my earlobes, and my fingers white with my body's chill. All I could do was lie there – only for about 15 seconds, though.

"Okay Little Beale," she announced after my short break. I don't have the time or money to take much more than a short break. "Let's go over to the Total Gym."

I enjoy the Total Gym so I didn't hesitate to sit up and move toward my chair. It was like all my Power-Plate-related stress disappeared when she said the words "Total Gym." Also when she calls me "Little Beale" I will cooperate with anything that follows. I think she knew that, too.

I transferred back into my wheelchair and rolled to the opposite side of the room. The Total Gym is made of a padded, sliding mat set on a frame that's held up diagonally from the floor. The bottom of the machine has a footplate to hold my legs, for me to push off from, and for a trainer to sit on. Needless to say, it's not an easy transfer.

Without a word and because we had been doing it for so many consecutive days, Laura came from behind and grabbed my legs simultaneous with me levitating my upper body onto the sliding mat. As routine, we did team work until my hips were aligned on the mat and legs secured on the footplate. She jammed a pillow between her butt and the thin plate then squatted down – I'm sure because a full sit would be too painful. Her hands rested on my kneecaps to keep them locked, and I started on two sets of 20 crunches. They were supposed to be crunches, at least.

Looking back to my earlier days in my disability, my angsty feelings toward therapists and trainers were justified; I had every right to be angry. I wasn't angry at them personally, I just had a hard time with my life situation. The truth? They were good. They tried hard to relate to me and make rehab fun, but my despondency wasn't an easy case to crack.

As I got older and more comfortable in my disability, though, my thoughts have matured. Instead of being overwhelmed and dampened by my inability, I have a need to overcome my circumstance. I'm comfortable with who I am at this point in my life, but that doesn't slow me down in wanting to improve myself and restore my body in every way possible. Laura is the first person I found who I felt truly, seriously understood that. That's only the first reason I love her.

"Okay Little Beale," Laura said after I crunched my body for the final repetition. "Next we're going to the parallel bars to work on your standing balance."

"Yes," I responded with a wave of energy and ultimate enthusiasm. "Okay." I love the flow of exercise where I have no time to rest or process much of anything until the end of the work out. It's better that way.

The parallel bars are my favorite and seemingly most practical exercise of all. Standing at parallel bars with a trainer locking my knees is the closest that I've gotten to walking as an able-bodied person since 2005, so it's easy to see why. Where the other exercises are important and indirectly bring me closer to my independence, standing at parallel bars allows me to see and remember what it's like to be a normal person again.

I transferred into the chair-height table, rolled to the middle of the bars, and positioned my toes against Laura's knees. I slid my body to the edge of my wheelchair cushion and took a nose full of air.

"Are you ready?" I asked. Excitement was leaking from every word I spoke.

"Almost," Laura said. She crouched to my feet and grabbed onto my kneecaps, preparing to hold them in locked position when I stood. "Okay now I'm ready."

I gripped the bars on either side of my breastbone and pushed up until my arms were fully extended. I readjusted my posture and hips to accommodate for weakness in my abdomen that causes my butt to stick out behind me like a hip hop dancer. This would be flattering for me if my butt wasn't as flat as a wooden board, but it definitely is. I won't look in the mirror until my body is even and I'm completely upright.

"Okay," I breathed. I unslumped my shoulders and stared through the glass office in front of me.

My upper back started to relax and I was able to settle my weight into my legs. I turned my head to the mirror on my right and scanned my nearly 6 foot tall body. My perspective standing up is drastically different than it is while sitting down, and something I would love nothing more than to get used to.

"Shift your weight to your left foot," Laura said from below me. "You're leaning."

I reweighted my body until she nodded her head and smiled in a way that makes my heart happy. We spent the next 30 minutes niggling at every imperfection in my standing posture, muscle weakness, and weight distribution. It's amazing how many things can be wrong with my body from standing stationary in parallel bars, and we scrutinized every one of them.

Not only am I going to walk one day, I'm going to look good doing it.

Before I wanted or expected, my muscles fatigued and my body crumpled onto the mat beneath me. This is a sign of a job well done and a worthwhile workout.

"That worked out perfectly," Laura stood up and said. She looked to me on the floor, the clock on the wall, and back to me again.

"Yes," was the only word I could force out of my mouth. I was tired.

I laid on the floor with a tomato-colored face, arms spread wide, and legs left however they landed from my crumble. I knew that my time in the middle of the floor was limited, so I had to savor every second before I had was inevitably told to sit up and be a normal person again. The gym was filling with other people and wheelchairs, and a body sprawled in the middle of the floor can't last long.

I laid there for 5 glorious seconds before I heard Angela greeting Mom walking in the door.

"Good timing," Angela said and turned to face my limp body on the ground. "Kristin is over there on the floor."

I poked my head toward my shoulder and saw Mom walking toward me with a wide smile on her face.

"Hey," she said with so much happiness in her voice. I would expect nothing less from my beach babe. "Did you have a good workout?"

I nodded my head, lifted my arm, and flopped it back to the floor.

"Hi Mom," Laura walked from her office and said. "She worked hard today."

They both looked down at me so I felt like I had to do something. I flopped my hand again.

"It looks like it," Mom piped. "Let's go eat lunch. Then we can walk to the shops and look around."

"Okay," I wiggled onto my elbows and said louder than I intended. "Let's go to that sandwich place over there." I turned my head pointedly toward the Design District.

"Okay," Mom said. "That's where I was thinking, too."

I transferred into my wheelchair and turned to look at Laura now with the most serious, businesslike expression I could make.

"I'm coming to work out at 2:00," I commanded. "Have a good lunch break."

"Bye Little Beale," she looked at me and smiled that smile again. It's the most genuine smile of anyone I know and one of the greatest reasons I love Awakenings and her so much. "Bye Momma Beale," she looked at Mom and said.

I turned my chair toward the door, hoping Mom would catch my hint and follow behind me. Without my noticing but probably while I was lying on the floor, the gym had filled up with familiar faces – dare I say friends. Everyone was busy doing their own thing and too much friendliness translates into a waste of money and a waste of valuable training time, so all I did was smile at them.

I wove myself through the maze of empty wheelchairs, bodies on the ground, and workout equipment until I reached Angela at the front desk.

"See you in two hours," I called to her, not stopping the momentum of my chair to the outside door and the California weather.

"Bye Beales," she called back with a smile that I could hear in her voice. "Have a good lunch. I'll see you at 2:00."

"I didn't come here for easy, Dad"

I don't know if it's teenagers today overall or just specific to Kristin, but the fighting spirit that I witness from her is outstanding. That was her response when we "spoke" (using IM) last night. I had asked her how she was feeling and mentioned that it was probably pretty tough on her the first week, but that it would get easier with time. It's statements like that and situations like hers that bring to light how small my "problems" are. Again, my 16 year-old is teaching this 45 year-old a thing or two.

Rhonda and Kristin are doing fine together. Rhonda says she feels like they're on an island; away from everyone with very little contact back home. Even though cell phones make it easy keep in touch, it's "out of sight, out of mind". Amid the heavy schedule, there are emotional times of frustration. Mentally, I think Kristin is in California doing what she wants to do, but in reality, she still has to do schoolwork. As soon as the morning workout is done, the tutor is actually waiting for her to return and go to work; not much of a break! Lunch is squeezed in between. When tutoring is done, she goes in for the afternoon workout. After dinner, they then go back to Awakenings to ride the FES bike for an hour. Then there is homework. I think Kristin's image of California has been burst with all this work! I don't know how she does it. She's taking Chemistry, Algebra II, and a new language – from the other side of the country.

She's not here for easy.

CHAPTER 15

Surfing

"**G**et ready," the man said and moved his hand to the side of my surf board. "You're taking the next wave."

"Am I supposed to do something?" I asked, confused and even kind of clueless. He had given me literally no instructions.

"No," he shouted back. "Just hold on and enjoy the ride."

At least that's what I think he said. He shoved my board into the waves before I heard the end of his sentence.

A few days earlier, I met a man at a bonfire at Moonlight Beach in Encinitas, California who is in a wheelchair and also a semi-professional adaptive surfer. The bonfire was an event put on by Awakenings Health Institute, the gym I was visiting, so I was in a happy company of other wheelchair users.

This guy was the coolest. He was telling about traveling the coast to surf and dropping the names of some beaches that I think should have impressed me, but I didn't recognize any. I either smiled big or gave him a slow nod for every one he mentioned, and that seemed to do the trick.

In the middle of telling me about an upcoming surfing competition in Hawaii, he suggested I learn to surf during my visit. My head nods must have been extra convincing.

"I would love to try it," I said. I spoke slowly and with obvious curiosity, even suspicion. "I'm always up for a new adaptive sport. Where and when?"

"Newport Beach," he told me. "It's close to Laguna Beach. The event is tomorrow."

I sat by the fire and listened to his stories of surfing adventures. Listening to him intrigued me and inevitably made me want to try adaptive surfing myself. Surfing is meant for people who can stand up. How in the world could I do it? I had to find out.

Sports were a huge part of my life before I got hurt and one of my biggest goals in rehabilitation: to be able to get up and run around like I used to. I miss being able to push myself physically and I miss not having a body as complicated as a physics problem. Physics or chemistry – take your pick. They're equally as complicated. I'm willing to try anything to get back the feeling of a tired body after playing sports.

After I got home from the bonfire, I told Mom and our new friend Cassandra about the surfing opportunity, then signed myself up for the event the next morning. It all happened very fast. Mom and Cassandra were as excited as I was.

The next morning came fast. My excitement woke me up one hour before the alarm clock went off, but had to stay quiet in bed until Mom got up. As soon as she did, though, I popped up and I was ready to go in record time. We met Cassandra in the parking lot of our hotel and the three of us drove 2 hours north to Newport Beach.

When we arrived, Mom parked the car next to a tent that was parallel to the parking lot and carried a banner with the words "Wheels2Water" written across it. If the sign wasn't enough of an indication we were in the right place, the 10 empty wheelchairs were a dead give-away. The three of us folded out of the car toward the tent, still not sure what to expect. As I rolled closer, I was immediately sucked in to the energy of the people inside.

"Hello and welcome to our surfing event," a man said without slowing his stride past me.

"What's your name?" a different man galloped up and asked. He held a pen in position, ready to scribble down what I said, then I assumed would run away. Sure enough, he wrote down my name, made some secret notes, and scuttled back to the tent.

The three of us stood in place and watched the commotion of happy people around us. Seconds later, a different man ran up to me with a clipboard in his hands. I felt like I was speed dating: men came, talked for a few seconds, and moved on to the next contestant.

"What size wetsuit do you think you need?" that third man asked.

"I need a small," I said enthusiastically – probably too much enthusiasm for a wet suit.

As soon as I spoke, he ran away and returned seconds later with two wetsuits in his hands. He looked at my body up and down then threw them both on my lap.

"I think these are both going to be too big for her," he said to a different, new man standing behind him. They were talking like I wasn't there. "We'll have to do the best we can."

Without a word spoken to me, the fourth man grabbed a plastic bag off a nearby table and jerked my leg off my wheelchair footplate. The bag confused me and, apparently, I showed that confusion in my expression. He looked at me, lingered for a moment on my face, and explained.

"It's hard to put on a wetsuit without these," he announced, motioning toward the bags. "We put these bags on your feet so they'll slide into the suit without catching."

I nodded because it's all I could do, really. I watched as he handled my legs like a bag of dried beans. He crammed my plastic-wrapped right foot into the leg hole then did the same for my left. Both of my legs slid into the wetsuit without any trouble. As predicted, once the wetsuit was fully zipped and buttoned, it hung off my body like a sweatshirt. No one said anything to me about it, though, so I guess that was okay.

The next step was getting me wet. I looked around and saw a beach wheelchair to help me to the water's edge. Honestly, I was hoping someone would just carry me into the water. A beach wheelchair has never failed to be an unpleasant experience and, as an attractive man rolled it toward me, I saw this time would be no different. With a rusted frame; a firm, unforgiving seat; awkwardly placed arm rests; and 20-inch-wide blowup tires, the chair takes every drop of independence away from its passenger.

But there was a positive side – there is always a positive side. The attractive man was standing next to the chair, waiting to lift my body and push me down the beach. Even if it's just for a transfer, I'm not one to reject an attractive man touching my body.

"You're going to have eight men helping you surf today," he told me as I rolled closer. "There will be two in the water with you to initiate your surf, and six others scattered along your path to the shore."

I turned my head to see all of the men standing in a group by the water. Every one of them was better looking than the next. It was amazing.

The original attractive man crammed one arm under both of my thighs and one arm around my lower back to load my body into the beach wheelchair. We were wasting no surf-time. He smiled a beautiful smile and we began the uncomfortable journey to the water's edge.

"Are you ready to get wet?" he asked from behind me when we finally approached the surf. Travel time in those chairs always felt twice as long.

I nodded my head, smiled, and he called over 3 more good looking men to help. They all shuffled behind me and worked together to ease my chair into the water. When the wet reached my toes, the chair came to a quick stop.

"I'll tilt your chair back so no water gets in your eye," one of the men explained and pushed me into the waves further from the shore. I don't know which man said it, but I had 4 good looking options so I couldn't lose.

"Okay," I responded at an inaudible volume. "Thank you."

Whoever was pushing tilted my chair on its back wheels and we went deeper into the water. The waves crashed all around me and went straight for my pupils. It was nice for him to try to protect me, but tilting the chair did nothing. The water was unreasonably cold and jumping at me with intention. I shut my eyes for protection.

When we arrived at a spot where the water began to cover my lap, the chair stopped. The men, standing in my every direction, looked down at me as if to say "We're done. Your ride is over."

I followed their unspoken instructions and slumped my body into the piercing cold water. I probably looked like a dead worm falling out of that chair. It was an awkward move to make.

Before I could process my next move, four men came from my all sides, grabbed my body, and slammed me chest down on a surf board. I didn't see who it was, but a voice coming from somewhere gave me my first instruction:

"Hold the handles in front of you and enjoy the ride."

I was still clueless and void of all responsibility, but at least I had a little bit of instruction.

In the same moment, two different men swam in front of me and yanked my board in the opposite direction. I turned my head as far to the right as my lifejacket would allow and saw the remaining 6 treading water behind us. I was surrounded.

The 6 trailing men dispersed themselves along my surfing path as I was being dragged deeper and deeper into the water. The man at my board's front kept attempting conversation, but the waves made it impossible to hear any of his words. The only thing I could do was follow his facial cues and guess when to smile and nod my head. This satisfied him enough until we reached neck-high water and we stopped moving. Again, I relied on body language to tell me that something was about to happen. He turned my board to face the shore, adjusted my feet, and swam into my vision.

"Get ready," he looked me in the eyes and shouted. "We're going to take this next one."

I nodded my head, gave him a weird looking smile, and showed him a small thumbs up. The waves were noisy and I didn't want to waste more surf-time with dialogue.

The wave came and he shoved my board into the beginning of its climb. I felt a smile spread all the way across my face as I glided across the water. I was accelerated by every current that followed behind me. The cold left my body and I was on top of the world. Back on the shore, Mom and Cassandra were jumping up and down and waving their arms in circles. I felt awesome and I can only hope someone caught my smile on camera.

Then, nose dive. My body flipped off the surfboard and smacked into the water in one fast second. As soon as my head was fully underneath, I took a sniff with my nose and opened my mouth; I wasted no time filling my body with children's urine, human saliva, sea-creature-discharge, and everything else I don't want to imagine.

Although it was only a couple of seconds, my time under the water felt like forever. Are the men ever going to come? Am I going to die before they get to me? Is this the end?

Much sooner than someone with a closed mouth, all air was gone from my lungs and my nostrils were on fire. Flailing arms are the only thing standing between a paraplegic and drowning, so that's what I did: I flung my arms in every direction until my nose reached the air, then I flung some more.

I finally fell into a somewhat comfortable rhythm of staying on top of the water when two strong arms swooped me up. I sighed with relief when I saw it was the arms of a handsome man and not the arms of death. Without a word, he slapped my body back onto the surf board and we glided over the next wave that was rolling toward us.

"Are you cold?" the new man asked.

"Very," I said through chattering teeth. "But not cold enough to go in." Despite my wipeout, I was having a lot of fun.

"All right," he said with a smile in his voice. "Let's go again."

He grabbed a handle on the top of my board to drag it further away from the shore and into the deep water.

We spent another hour and a half in the ocean until I was finally surfing all the way to the shore without wiping out. I was quickly gaining surfing-confidence while having a ton of fun. My body was still very cold, but there were too many distractions for me to notice or care. As I surfed down the path and past the men, they shouted "You're a natural!" and "You're killing it!" I was on top of the world again.

The last wave I caught was a big one. Honestly, I think they pushed me into it too early, but that might just be me looking for someone to blame. My board caught the side of the wave and my body plunged off the front and into the ocean in another fast second. Immediately after I landed in the water it came shooting back at me, clocked me in my nose, and left me floating, shocked, and confused.

Three men showed up next to me within seconds and, again, swooped me out of the water. This time they had concern on their faces.

"Are you okay?" one of the men swam close and asked, invading my personal space. "It looked like the board got you right in the face."

"Yes I'm fine," I said, my voice now sounding like I had a head cold. "It hit me in the nose hard."

"We'll call it a day," he said without hesitation. "You're shaking pretty badly from the cold water."

I nodded and allowed myself to be carried to the shore. I wasn't completely sold in "calling it a day," but I suspected the men were tired and looking for an excuse to go in, so I let it happen.

After the excitement of surfing went away and the men pushed my board to the shore, I realized that I was in fact really, very cold. My nose was starting to burn and my wetsuit was uncomfortable. My fingers were white and my teeth chattered at high speeds.

As we swam in, I watched Mom and Cassandra smiling and jumping on the shore. Just that visual made every pain and shiver of my body worth it. I pushed my body up on my elbows in a position of superiority and glided toward the beach.

Moments like these are what makes the uninteresting, repetitive workouts worth it. Slowly and in a different way than I would have expected, I was getting back into who I used to be. The familiar euphoria of a successful workout, in whatever form, was and is one of the only things keeping me sane. I had something to be proud of and something to distract myself away from my disability.

We reached shallow water, the men swarmed around with a towel and a wheelchair transfer, and I smiled in the thought that now I can say I'm a surfer – an adaptive surfer, even better. I probably won't have the opportunity to surf again, but I'll hang on to that title.

Kristin is wasting no time taking every opportunity to do as much as she can with no fear. While in California, she went surfing. Fresh off that experience, she said, "They're putting together a surfing trip to Costa Rica in November. What do you think about me going?"

This from going surfing ONE time. I have a little adrenaline junkie working here. "When is it?"

"2nd week in November."

"Um, does SCHOOL or GPA mean anything to you?" I laughed.

"Oh. Good point. I guess that's important, too."

3 hours later...."Hey Dad, I'm thinking about trying tennis..."

It's always "go time" with her.

CHAPTER 16

Kennedy Krieger

"Did you wake up last night?" Mom leaned over my bed from the reclining chair she slept on and asked in a whisper.

"Yes," I answered with frustration in my voice that was probably obvious also by looking at my face. "At least four times."

When we arrived at Johns Hopkins Hospital one week earlier, Mom and I had the perfect accommodation: a newly renovated room, no roommate, and a nurse's station outside our door to get us anything we asked for. My insurance paid for rehabilitation for two weeks and, since we had exhausted our cross-country-options for the time being, we jumped on the opportunity to try somewhere new and closer to home: The Kennedy Krieger Institute in Baltimore, Maryland.

> *Yet again, we are trying something new. Soon after arriving at Kennedy Krieger, Kristin was analyzed. The results of her test reveal that she has an ASIA B/Incomplete injury. That is a very good thing – Kristin's hard work in California and back home took her from a Complete (no chance of recovery) to Incomplete (chance of recovery). This is very big news.*
>
> *This facility is not nearly as appealing as San Diego, but I feel certain it is better in terms of their qualifications. Unfortunately it does feel like we're back in Children's Hospital, so I can see why she isn't as excited. She feels like being inpatient in another hospital is taking a step backwards.*
>
> *That being said, it is the epicenter of research for spinal cord injury recovery. Our ability to get Kristin into their program, get them to know Kristin personally, etc. will perhaps be a benefit when a cure for spinal cord injury begins human trials.*

A couple days after arriving at the facility and after getting comfortable in our unfamiliar but nearly-ideal environment, we were introduced to our first roommate, Amy. When I say "introduced" I mean the nurses told us about her arrival, then the next day she was there, sleeping in the corner bed, when we returned from therapy.

They told us – warned us – that Amy is a seventeen year old girl with "brain storms." At first I was excited because I thought our new roommate was going to be full of original ideas, but I quickly learned that Amy's brain storms are not anywhere close to that; her "storms" didn't mean that she is a creative person, rather that the processes in her mind are mixed in a way that causes her uncontrollable and constant outbursts. Needless to say, I was bummed.

Not long after Amy moved in, we heard the first crack of thunder. She screamed, sang, and shrieked at the top of her lungs and at all times of the day and night. It was consistent and, to my naivety, unbelievable.

I couldn't fathom why the nursing staff chose me and my sweet mother to share a room with her.

"Kevin got run over by a school bus and it happened at Kennedy Krieger but I did not push him," she screamed without pausing. Nothing ever made sense. "Stanley. I love Stanley. I wish I could come Stanley, but I am too fat. It's not fair, Stanley."

Then she sang the Star Spangled Banner.

For the first hours it was funny, in a guilty kind of way. It was funny in the times that Mom and I had the option of leaving the room and her behind us. But as the day neared end and I needed to sleep to forget where I was for some hours, the songs and outbursts lost their humor.

Only two days of avoiding our room and functioning on minimal sleep went by until Mom and I put in a request for relocation. Quicker than I expected and probably thanks to empathy from the nurses, our request was approved to move to a different room – "soon." They didn't tell us when, but knowing it was coming was good enough. We were ready for a new adventure.

The next morning served as evidence to how much smoother we could move when we had something to look forward to; when motivated, Mom and I are like a well-oiled machine. We knew we had good things ahead of us: our own room, a full night's sleep, and at least one moment of silence. That morning was easy, mainly because Amy was finally asleep.

I ate a full plate of crunchy eggs from the cafeteria, checked to see that Mom was finished eating her yogurt, and we made our way to the P.T gym. Somehow, on time. At Kennedy Krieger, it's to everyone's benefit to arrive within the minute of scheduled therapies, because your therapist will not hesitate to come to your room and escort/drag you to the therapy room. That's another disadvantage of being an inpatient and the only motivation I can think of to being at therapy on time.

I waved "goodbye" to Mom and took my last deep inhale before rolling through the door's threshold and into the foul-smelling room. The gym was as big as my bedroom but somehow had an average capacity of five to six patients plus their therapists. There were three mats on the floor with 1-2 people on each, two bikes, and one treadmill. It reminded me of a lot SCI Step, the gym I went to in Ohio. It was tight.

"Good morning," said Therese, my physical therapist. "Get on the mat and I'll be there in a second."

Therese was a middle aged woman with graying hair who, no matter what she was doing, was always sweating at both of her armpits, forehead, and under-boob. Her voice was quiet and her hands were soft as a dinner roll. She was a nice, though, so we worked well together.

I rolled my wheelchair next to the mat and transferred onto the edge.

"What game do you want to play today?" she appeared beside me moments later and asked. "I was thinking that we can play a game while balancing on the ball."

I still wasn't convinced game-playing is a thing to do while working out but, in this gym, it's a given. It wasn't rare to see someone lifting weights or balancing on a Dyna-disc while moving a game pawn across a board on the floor; exercises were completed with the incentive of making the next move. Actually, it was strange to see a client without a stack of board-game-options on the gym floor next to him or her. I tried to decline at first, but my request was overlooked so many times that I finally just gave in and played Clue.

My workouts at Kennedy Krieger were physically unchallenging and I grew bored of winning games against therapists who don't use common sense in their game play. That's how this particular therapy session was going. After one hour and two victorious rounds, Therese looked up at me in defeat.

"I have a meeting to go to," she blurted. "You can spend the next hour with Colleen." She stood up and motioned toward a girl in her late twenties standing in the doorway. "I'll see you tomorrow."

"She was tired of losing," I thought and watched her slump away from me. One hour per day is apparently all it takes for me to get sucked in to the board-game-mentality of that place. I was more concerned with winning the games than I was with my "workout."

I turned my head back around and saw Colleen standing over me with a box in her hand, smile on her face. As she walked closer, I realized she is also one of the most beautiful people I had seen since I got there. For some reason that made me feel a little better.

"I thought we could stay on the ball and play a new game," she proudly announced. "This one's my favorite. It's called Blokus."

She opened the box and pulled out a square board and 2 handfuls of different colored and shaped game pieces. She extended one hand and let go of what looked like 30 pieces, falling to the ground like a waterfall.

"You have this blue piece so you go first," she pointed to a blue triangle and explained. "Then I put down a piece that matches yours until the board is full."

For the next 5 precious minutes of my workout Colleen detailed the game of Blokus to me. My time was being wasted but, at this point, I didn't mind at all. Seriously not at all.

"You can move your own pieces as long as you keep your balance while you bend over," Colleen bargained. "Let's get on the table." She moved a foam cube to clear a space for me to sit. "Come on. Quick like a bunny."

She spoke in a slightly elevated voice that made me feel like either a dog or a small child, and told me to be a bunny after nearly every command. But I liked her. Although not much, I got the most benefit from my time with Colleen than with any of the women I worked with at that gym. Still, by the end of PT, I felt more confident in my Blokus skills than my core muscles.

My therapy session ended and I rolled slowly back to my hospital room. I came in the door and saw Amy still sleeping and Mom in the corner talking on her cell phone. When I rolled in the room she saw me, smiled, and waved her hand to come over.

"Yeah," she half-whispered to the mystery person on the other end. "She just came in the room. I'll let you talk to her." Mom held out the phone in her hand for me to take. "It's Judy."

"Hi Judy," I put it up to my ear and said. The volume of my voice had no concern for the sleeping Amy. I was excited to talk to someone from the outside of that hospital building. Even better, someone from home.

"What's going on?" she asked. I appreciated her question even though she most likely knew every exaggerated detail from Mom.

"I just got back from PT," I rehearsed. "We played a new game called Blokus and it was good. I won a couple of times."

"What is that noise in the background?" Judy asked with some frustration in her voice. Amy had woken up and started singing Amazing Grace.

"That's our new roommate," I half-shouted. Amy was getting louder.

"I can hardly hear you," Judy fully-shouted back. "It's annoying. Call me later. I can't talk with that in the background."

"Bye," I said. I accepted my Amy-induced telephone defeat.

Mom walked around to Amy's machines to look for an OFF or mute button. Added to the song, her machines were beeping loudly and consistently. She searched for 1-2 minutes before a nurse slowly walked in and lazily pushed buttons on Amy's machine. The beeping stopped. The nurse scribbled notes on a clipboard and turned to us. Her dropping eyes made it look like she could fall over at any moment. Was she very tired or almost dead? I couldn't tell.

"We have another room you can move into down the hall," she slurred. "It has two other kids in it but they don't talk. One of them is leaving tomorrow afternoon."

Mom and I didn't hear the second sentence because we were already grabbing our luggage and walking out the door. The other reason we didn't hear her is because Amy had jumped into a chorus of "The Wind Beneath My Wings."

The two of us, like kids loading onto the van for a field trip, followed closely behind the nurse to our new room. I was excited to see that it was bigger and nicer than the last 2 rooms because it was designed to accommodate three people.

There was a girl, whose name tag said Nekayla, who looked no older than 11 years. There was another lady, I assumed her mother, who was balancing on a stack of pillows in a chair next to her – a bed to sleep on just like Mom had. For some reason that gave me a spark of hope.

The spark died after we were in the room for 5 minutes and she didn't say one word to us. Her eyes were zoned into the TV and she had no apparent interest in a friendship, so we let that be.

The other body in the room was a young boy, probably also 11 years old, who was also glued to the television. I didn't bother to ask his name because he was leaving the following afternoon. He didn't seem to care for us much either, so I made no effort. Evidently friends are hard to come by at Kennedy Krieger.

Even though it was better than being in the room with Amy, the first night in our new room was, again, very hard. The boy screamed at nothing in the same way I've heard people scream when they're being murdered in horror movies. Nekayla's machines beeped at a damaging volume that everyone could hear except for the nurses, I guess. Her mother slept through everything. We found out later that she went to a bar and got drunk every night before bed so she could sleep through the commotion of her child without having to deal with it. Great.

The chaos was only registered by me and Mom. "Chaos" is a good word. We were the only people left to suffer through it.

Mom met me at the door of the physical therapy gym the next morning and we returned to our room with a surprise was waiting for us. It was no surprise that Nekayla was lying in the corner with her TV on full volume and her mom sleeping on the chair beside her, but that there were two new bodies in our room: a teenaged black girl and her mother. From what I could tell of their outward appearances, they seemed like normal folks. If this trip taught me anything, though, it taught me to not set my hopes too high in regards to people's normalcy.

"Hi," the girl said one second after I rolled in. "My name is Courtney and I'm here because I had a stroke when I was a baby. I'm 17 now but I still have trouble walking sometimes."

I was a little surprised by her rush of personal information, but also grateful. I liked it. Finally there was someone who talked instead of screamed. Finally there was someone who was not hooked up to 10 beeping machines.

Three more minutes and I was armed with the nearly complete story of Courtney's life. My and Courtney's moms talked about adult things, and Courtney and I were becoming friends at a rapid pace. I was finally, finally making a friend.

After all the excitement of introductions died off, my tired body resurfaced and slapped me in the face. It was more like a punch. The hospital drained my energy and, I realized when I saw her putting on pajamas at 8:45pm, Mom felt the same way. I got myself ready for bed, transferred into my hard cot, and everyone in the room was asleep within an hour. Nekayla was finally in the background.

The next day at therapy was great and I felt fulfilled. It wasn't great because I made progress or overcame a challenge in physical therapy, but it was great because I beat Colleen in Blokus, Life, and Clue. Rightfully so, I felt like a champion when I met Mom at the end of my workout to return to our roommates – or so we thought.

A nurse met us in the hallway in front of our door even before we had a chance to open it.

"Nekayla and her mother requested to be moved to a new room," she said. "They moved out while you were in PT."

I was confused and even a little offended by Nekayla's rejection, but mostly relieved.

Mom opened the room's door and I saw that the nurses had already changed it from the crowded, disorganized mess of beeping equipment, to just me, Courtney, and our moms. Things were going to get better – I could tell.

The rest of my stay went by fairly quickly. It's amazing the difference a full night of sleep and a friend makes. I quickly learned that Blokus was not only Colleen's favorite game, but everyone's favorite game; I must have played it four times per one-hour therapy session. If nothing else, the hours I spent in PT were worthwhile because I became a champion Blokus player.

Two weeks spent as an inpatient at Kennedy Krieger seemed to last one year. With the end of the second week approaching, I was excited to get away from the hospital, the board games, and the floating plate of stale eggs at my door every morning. My list of rehabilitative gains from my stay is a little bit obscured, but I'm happy to have the experience. I had the opportunity briefly to meet with John McDonald, who was Christopher Reeves' doctor and the creator of a game-changing therapeutic bike, so that was cool and moderately beneficial.

The therapy Kristin is receiving at Kennedy Krieger is somewhat different than what we have been instructed to do by Project Walk and the other places we've visited. We are receiving more positive results, though. We are getting individual attention from Dr. MacDonald, which we believe to be cutting edge advice on spinal cord injuries. Getting accepted into KKI was nothing short of an act of congress, so we want to exploit all the time we can possibly get with insurance approval. It's not comfortable for us, but certainly worthwhile.

For patients with disabilities of a higher severity and a younger age, Kennedy Krieger Institute an ideal spot. For me, it's a good story to tell.

CHAPTER 17

Dominican

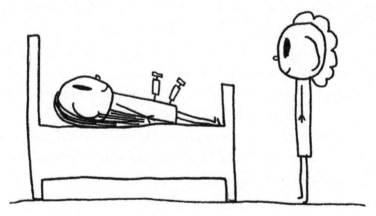

Terrifying is a good word. I was terrified.

Mom and I were at the end of a three day long, mid-January vacation to the Dominican Republic. The purpose of our trip was for me to receive stem cells – rumored to help countless human conditions, namely the return of sensation and/or function in victims of paralysis. The potential of those cells is incredible and, as you may know by now, the answer to almost every single one of my prayers.

There are umbilical cord stem cell treatments being done constantly. This treatment is not nearly as controversial as embryonic. We are narrowing our conversations to consider this trip. Kristin always finds a way to slip that into most conversations; e.g., "We can't do that on the 4th of July because we'll be in China." She says that with a smirk and a smile. How can a father deny a daughter when she looks at you with yearning in her eyes and a smile on her face? If I would give all that I own to see her walk, fall in love, have children....live a full life, why not take a chance, right?

We learned about the cells three weeks earlier from an article that detailed the enormous returns of a girl close to my age with a similar injury level. I showed the article to my parents, we did the appropriate research, and were on an airplane to the Dominican Republic less than one month later. The motto is to "leave no stone unturned," and I have a pretty good record of following suit.

Now, Mom and I were riding in a maroon minivan from our hotel to the Santo Domingo airport in Dominican. Our driver was a native-speaking man wearing a torn camisole. He wove in and out of traffic, ignored signs, needlessly honked his horn, and spoke to us at a deafening volume. I was scared for my life.

Traffic laws in the Dominican Republic differ significantly from those in the United States: our laws are enforced and their laws are actually just advice. My experience of driving from the airport at the beginning of the trip was enough to tell me that car horns exist for the purpose of background music, you only sometimes need to drive on the right side of the road, and there is no punishment for not taking the "advice" of speed limits and road markings. The continual beat of the horn lost all significance to me by the time we merged onto the highway. It truly was in the background.

With a working speedometer and a different driver, I anticipated the van ride back to the airport to have potential for our safer transfer. Not long until those hopes were shattered, though. I'm not smart enough to convert km to mph, but I am smart enough to know that driving 130km in an area with an 80km speed limit is considered reckless. My first Dominican-driving-experience included tailgating and weaving between cars, and my second promised driving in the middle of the road and traveling at reckless speeds.

"How do you say 'scared' in Spanish?" Mom asked as a motorcycle sped in front of us and avoided collision by few inches. She was sitting in front seat with our driver, Fabio, and I was in the back seat grabbing the door handle for dear life.

"Asustado," responded Fabio with exploding laughter.

It seemed like he recognized Mom's weak humor, but chose to overlook the legitimate and serious concern that was tucked inside. I watched as he closed his eyes, bent over in laughter, and banged his fists on the steering wheel. I was literally living my nightmare.

"Beautiful ladies go to airport," Fabio confirmed and jammed his fist into Mom's shoulder. She gave a weak smile and head nod.

Every third sentence he spoke, Fabio reached across the van and jabbed Mom on her arm with his fist like two old friends sharing stories. Mom made a weird laughing noise and maintained an unnatural expression every time he touched her. It made more sense to play along with him because he was, in fact, behind the wheel and we didn't want to give him any more reason to lose control.

The Spanish music was unnecessarily loud and our bodies were being tossed around like a bag of onions. Trying to distract my mind, I strained for their conversation and jumped on every opportunity to contribute, if only just a snort. The combination of his strong accent, the music, and the beeping car horns meant that's all I really did, though: snort. I couldn't make out anything they were saying.

All the sudden Fabio's unnecessarily loud cell phone ringtone blared from the center console. I could definitely hear that. He heard it too and went into frenzy, letting go of the steering wheel and searching the console with both hands. Not quickly enough, he pulled it from a pile of crumpled papers and wrappers, pushed a button on the keypad, and the van swerved into the oncoming lane. He calmly reached down and turned down the music before correcting our van on the road. Meanwhile, I was hyperventilating.

Even from the back seat, I could hear a man on the other end of the phone talking with a strong and fast Spanish accent. Fabio immediately started telling what I guessed was an emotional story because he used both of his hands while he spoke: one holding the phone and the other waving in the air to accentuate his words. I watched from the back of the van in horror.

"You have pen and paper?" he turned his whole face toward me in the back seat and asked. The phone was still smashed against his ear. "I give you number and you call when you come back."

Realizing he might not turn around until I found something, I grabbed a pen and a scratch of paper from the floorboard as quickly as I could. He took his phone away from his ear with one hand, pushed a button with his other, and at this point had completely given up looking at the road.

"Three, seven, six," he said, looking at me still. "Pie loo mune jan."

I couldn't understand him so I drew triangles folded the paper in my lap. If I could help it, I will never get in Fabio's van again.

"I'm going to tell my husband I hung out with Fabio in the Dominican Republic," Mom announced. Fabio beeped the horn and look at her, confused. "That's a sexy model in America," she clarified when nobody laughed.

She smiled to herself, content with her failed joke. He beeped the horn two more times and continued in his reckless speed down the road.

The whole reason Mom and I were in the Dominican Republic was so I could have stem cell therapy. The day before, I received stem cells in a process drastically different than I imagined. Because of the still experimental status of research with stem cells in the United States, I imagined there would be men in ninja-like costumes that would throw me and Mom over their shoulders and climb up the walls to a secret room on the balcony where I they would give me silver liquid through a long needle. Or something like that. I let my imagination go a little bit wild.

The reality was a navy minivan driven by a hairy man that dropped us off at a house that looked very similar to my own. I laid on a normal-looking bed, was stuck by 2 normal-looking needles, then was told to "rest" for one normal hour. One needle [located in my lower abdomen] was flushing me with saline, while the other needle [located near my right oblique muscle] was transferring thousands of stem cells into my body. I waited on the bed for 45 minutes after my injection and chatted with Mom until a nurse came in to take the needles out. She told me I should start seeing results of the stem cells in 6-8 months, manifesting in new movement, new sensation, or countless other alternatives. The benefit of the cells had the potential to be enormous or, on the flip side, very tiny. That's the risk I was taking.

With no warning, my neck and head snapped forward as our minivan screeched into the loading station of JetBlue. He almost literally tore me from my thoughts.

Fabio instantly spun around in his seat and gave us a smile that showed all of his teeth. It was nauseating.

"We here," he announced. "Bab chewbani lasso."

I think that's what he said. The combination of his rotten teeth and broken English made it very difficult to understand his words.

Fabio jumped out of the van, ran around it at full speed, unlocked my door, and stared at me for one half second. Before I could process what was happening, Fabio's arm was around my waist, his other arm under my thighs, and he dropped my body into my wheelchair seat. I didn't even see how my wheelchair got there.

In the same minute of putting me back in my chair, Fabio danced around to the trunk and motioned his hands toward our things – I guess to offer his assistance. Mom gave him a wide-eyed nod of her head and he picked up our bags with his skinny arms. Mom and I went toward the airport doors and he followed closely behind us, slammed our bags down as soon as we reached air conditioning, and smiled the same rotten smile. He was overwhelming.

"How much should we pay you for the ride?" Mom asked, holding a small pile of foreign bills.

"You decide," he said and smiled again with what I guessed was his most charming. Then he ran to the other side of the van to close the door. I wouldn't be surprised if I saw him peeking at us from a corner somewhere.

Mom picked out a handful of unrecognizable bills and held them out to me.

"You go give it to him," she tried.

"No way," I fought back. "He likes you. You have to do it."

Fabio must have overheard us or smelled the money because he appeared out of nowhere, standing over us with a big, greedy smile on his face.

"I deserve eighty dollars for dealing with you," he said. He thought he was funny. "Cough it up."

Mom made a weak smile and gave him only what he initially quoted. The three of us stood and stared at each other for few, uncomfortable moments.

"All right Fabio," I blurted to break the silence. "See you later."

I turned to the ramp and started rolling toward the check-in concierge. Mom followed behind me like a duckling.

"Adios," Fabio called out in his last attempt to connect.

Once I was on the platform I turned to look at him one last time.

"See you never," I whispered under my breath.

CHAPTER 18

Open Sea

There are just some things that bring us closer to where we need to be in life…sounds, smells, memories (good and bad), even the way something tastes. "Simple" is usually a common thread. Today Kristin and I were able to go on an adventure on our boat. This is the same boat that I cherish the fond memories of Jessica, Kristin, and Rhonda dancing on an evening cruise to songs by Earth Wind and Fire. Simply watching them hold each other in the chill of the wind, listening to John Mayer or James Taylor with a full moon or sunset in the background. Those memories mean so much to me.

"Are you ready to go?" Dad asked and walked through the door of my bedroom.

I was wearing so many layers I could hardly move; my body was wrapped tightly in two t-shirts, a Randolph-Macon College sweatshirt, an ugly wool sweater that Mom found in the attic, and a puffy winter jacket. I also had on gloves, two scarves, and a raccoon hat. Still, I knew the trip was going to freeze me.

"I'm ready but you're not," I said and rolled around the corner from the bathroom. There was Dad in an outfit of camouflage turtleneck, a camouflage sweatshirt, black inflatable pants, and a black beanie hat. He looked only slightly less ridiculous than me. "You're dressed like you're going hunting. Your body is going to be frozen, Dad."

"I'll be fine," he said with a puffed chest. He tucked his ridiculous turtleneck into his pants. "Are you ready?"

"Yes," I said. My voice was muffled by my 2 scarves and I couldn't move my neck, so I turned my whole body to look him in his eyes. "I'm ready as I'm going to be."

Dad sprinted behind me, grabbed the handlebars of my wheelchair, and popped me into a wheelie to roll through the grass that led to the dock.

"Okay," I said. Dad put my chair down from its wheelie when we arrived at the wooden dock by the water. I rolled forward to sit next to the boat. "I got water bottles and crackers in case we get hungry. They're in this bag that I'll put in the center console."

Dad grabbed his gloves from the equipment bag, jumped in the boat, and straight to the dashboard to push buttons. I don't think he was listening to me. "I charged my cell phone and packed extra blankets for when we get cold."

He was definitely not listening. I was excited and talking was the only thing I can do to keep from transferring out of my chair and log-rolling all the way to the captain's seat.

"Let's load her on the boat," Mom walked from behind us and said. "We need to tie down her wheelchair so it won't fly out."

Dad stepped away from his buttons and to the outside edge of the boat.

"Okay," he said and held both of his hands up to spot my next move. "Let's get you in here."

I let my torso fall over my thighs, both hands next to my feet, and eased myself to the ground – a transfer that took me long time to master at the beginning of my disability. Transferring in general took me a long time to master, but to and from the floor is next level difficulty.

My butt landed gently on the ground and I scooted to sit to the side of the dock with my legs hanging off the side. Dad scooped up my body and put me in the passenger seat next to the steering wheel. Mom lifted my wheelchair from where it sat on the dock, eased it into the boat, then tied it down with a rope.

As soon as my butt hit the seat's cushion and as soon as my wheelchair was secure, Mom skipped over to me with a rough-looking wool blanket in her arms. The wool blanket and my ugly wool sweater looked like they came together in a pack at Costco. She grabbed my legs, propped them on the dashboard, and wrapped them tightly in the blanket – probably costing me some circulation.

"Are you warm?" she asked with an anxious tone and overly eager expression. "Is there anything else I can get you?"

Again, I moved my whole torso to look at her.

"I'm doing well," I said with an unnaturally peppy voice – an attempt to restore some confidence. "Thank you, though."

She kissed me on a sliver of face that wasn't covered by my scarves and raccoon hat, and clambered back to the dock. Dad grabbed a handful of rope and began to untie the boat.

"Ooh," Mom burst. "Do you want sunglasses? I'll get you some sunglasses. Hold on."

Before I could process what she said or respond to her, she turned around and was skipping up the lawn to the house. She ran the whole way there and the whole way back. Dad and I laughed because she looked silly, but mostly so cute.

In a record two minutes later she was standing on the dock with a pair of my grandmother's sunglasses in her hand. My bulky outfit, those sunglasses, and lack of range in my upper body (from the layers) promised me I wouldn't be picking up any attractive men along the way. That was no surprise to me.

"Look," Mom held up the glasses and proudly announced. "They're Tommy Hill-finger."

"Thank you Mom," I said with secret laughter on my face. "Drive safely and I love you."

Dad pushed more buttons on the dashboard and the boat started to creep away from the land. Mom picked up Cody and waved his paw at us.

"Wave at me until I'm out of sight," she yelled to us on the boat in her cutest voice.

I started waving...and waving...and waving until Dad turned the boat around the corner and she was out of sight.

We were on the adventure of driving his boat from our house in Kilmarnock, VA all the way to Virginia Beach, VA for repairs and body work. At the same time, Mom and the dog were driving in the car to meet us and carry our likely ice-cubed bodies back home. The trip was predicted to take three hours on the bitter cold ocean, the Open Sea, and the conditions were supposed to be rough. I was thrilled.

I call it the Open Sea because no land can be seen from all sides; there are no barriers or immediate rules to follow – just open water. The main reason I agreed to be the co-captain on this trip is the sensation of being on a boat in the middle of the ocean is a feeling of complete freedom. Not only freedom, either. There's definitely some happiness, usually frigidity, and most of all an ability to abandon my wheelchair. The water was ice and my body was numb, but I was happy. Being in the Open Sea with my dad, my best friend, is even better.

When Kristin was in the hospital right after her accident, I made a deal. It was gently whispered in her ear, but quickly lodged in her mind as

I have been reminded of it on more than one occasion. "Kristin, I hope you can hear me. If you pull through this, I will take you on the "Open Sea" anytime you want and we'll go as fast as you want. Anytime. You just have to stay alive." There were times on our boat when we would troll along at dusk with a glass of wine and soft music. The girls would grow bored pretty quickly and Kristin would always try to encourage me to put it in high gear and hit the "Open Sea", which was the Chesapeake Bay or the Atlantic. More often than not, I would cave to her request.

Our boat was finally facing away from the land and my attention turned to the water ahead of us. I got into a position to enjoy the ride: one hand wrapped in the blanket and the other partly in front of me, ready to grab hold of the armrest and brace myself for a wave at any moment. Dad picked up speed and I watched the stick on the speedometer rise. The wind started to bite my nose and swell my cheeks, and I felt happy.

For the next hours my body was curled into a ball in the passenger seat. Occasionally Dad would look over to me and I would flash him an energetic smile. It was forced, yes, but not because I wasn't having a ton of fun. Smiling naturally is a luxury that goes away when nearly all body warmth has left and replaced by icy wind shooting up your nose. For three hours.

Dad and I spent that time in silence, exchanging only a few words due to the noise of the wind and waves. The weather report said that there would be 1-2 foot waves with 10-15 knot winds, but the reality was 3-4 foot waves with 20-25 knot winds. Also it felt like the maximum temperature hit no more than 35 degrees. The combination of waves, wind, and the speed of the boat let us ride airborne more than a few times.

"TURKEY," I heard Dad shout. "GREEN BASEBALLS."

I couldn't make out anything he was saying. But that's okay – I just smiled.

I was looking forward to 2 hours of quality time alone with Kristin and her smiling face. Rhonda bundled her up next to the Captain's seat with her famous Raccoon hat. She looked like she couldn't move even if she wanted to. Me, in full camo. We looked like misfits.

Am I complaining? Not at all. I was outside, on the water and the best part is every time I looked at Kristin, her face told it all. She was happy and when she caught me looking, she always smiled at me. We didn't talk much because it was so rough and the wind was loud. We even saw dolphin. I escaped the world with Kristin by my side for 2 hours. It did my heart good. I thanked God for that time and remembered where I was years ago in an ICU with a comatose daughter in front of me, praying and cutting deals and praying and praying and praying....

I may have mentioned this before, but Kristin always wanted to "go to the Open Sea" on the boat when all we were planning on doing was going to a waterside restaurant for dinner. "Not enough time tonight, sweetie, we're going to go back to the house. It's getting late." I said that too many times. What a fool for denying such a simple pleasure. Then, just 6 weeks ago, I find myself leaning over her bed praying she wouldn't die and promising her that I would take her to "the Open Sea" anytime she wants, but please don't leave us. Don't die. In my mind, she is ON the open sea every minute of every day. The fact that she's handicapped doesn't even matter to her. I'm just so unbelievably thankful that she's still in our lives.

As we got closer to Virginia Beach, I started to recognize landmarks from when we owned beach property in my childhood; I was weirdly nostalgic as we rode past memories of the area. The property that my parents sold in Virginia Beach is a polar opposite to the property they bought in Kilmarnock: Virginia Beach is filled with tourist spots and things to do, while Kilmarnock is full of old people, churches, and antique stores. It was a pretty dramatic change but I guess it was time for change as they got older. Ugh.

After about 2 hours, Dad slowed the boat down to a "No Wake Zone" and I began to breathe again. I looked around and saw the marinas and seaside shops that I spent so much time in when I was a kid. I saw the familiar beaches and roads I played on (the beaches, not the roads), and the restaurants my family occupied in the summer months.

The No Wake Zone led us to a marina, to my delight. Dad turned the boat toward the dock, parked next to a wooden pole in the water and, like always, started pushing buttons.

"I'm going to let you off here and go and park the boat over there," he said and pointed somewhere over my head. He pushed some final buttons then started pulling pieces of my wheelchair from the lower cabin. "Mom should be here soon."

I watched him, thanked God for keeping us safe, and said a quick prayer that Mom and Cody were safe. Also that they would hurry up.

"All right," Dad walked to the front of the boat and shouted to me. I looked up and saw him walking toward me with his hands out, prepared to grab my body. "Are you ready? Come here."

"Are you sure you can transfer me by yourself?" I asked with unmasked concern. I forgot to adjust my voice, so it was also kind of a scream. "Usually Mom is here to help."

"Yes," he said with a look in his eyes I recognized. It was a look that said "I'm a man. I can do this by myself."

I wrapped my arms around his neck and he picked me up to plop me back on the side of the boat. I grabbed my legs and swung them around to face outward over the water. From there, I transferred onto the dock and into my wheelchair to wait for my next instruction. We had done an out-of-boat-transfer countless times until it was finally smooth and thoughtless.

"Okay," he said. He pointed his finger to a spot on the land 100ft behind me. "Do you see that yellow line? Meet me right there and I'm going park the boat in the spot by the grass."

"Okay," I said and smiled. My body was finally starting to warm up.

I rolled to the yellow line and watched Dad push buttons on the boat again. He was standing next to the steering wheel in a black beanie, camouflage turtleneck, black inflatable pants, and camouflage sweatshirt hanging over his shoulder. His outfit was a sight that only a daughter and a committed wife could love.

I really wasn't one to talk though. I was the one sitting alone on the dock, in a wheelchair, wearing a raccoon hat, Gran's sunglasses on my head, and a wool sweater that looked like it's from a nursing home and feels like it's from the briar patch.

"Do you need help with anything?" I offered in a shout. I'm aware there's very little I can do from where I sat on the dock, but it's always nice to ask. Maybe he had a drink or a pamphlet I could hold.

"Nope," he said. "I'm done." He climbed out of the boat and walked over to me. "Mom is right over there."

I turned around and saw Mom sitting in her car in the parking lot with a pleasant smile on her face. When she saw the two of us she opened the door, speed-walked over, and started with questions.

"Hi," she said with a rushed tone. "Were you cold? How was the weather? Was it windy? Are you glad you wore sunglasses?" I looked at Dad and he was nodding his head "yes" to all questions. "Cody and I listened to a book on tape. I'm almost done with it."

I smiled. Cody is deaf.

Dad talked to a marina employee before we left, signed some papers, and the three of us loaded into the car. As soon as Mom cranked on the engine, the voice of a monotone narrator filled our heads. Before switching it off, I heard the end of Cooper's testimony to the murder of Francis. Patsy is not guilty after all.

"Where are we going to lunch?" I clicked off the stereo and asked once everyone was loaded in the car. My stomach was empty and it was the only thing I could process.

"I was thinking Bubba's," Mom said with a smile on her face. "I'm craving one of their crab cakes."

CHAPTER 19

Randolph-Macon College

College was a hard time for me. Even with all the pain and hardship that came with and after my accident, freshman year in college was the lowest time of my life.

When I was a senior year in high school, I only applied to one school: Randolph-Macon College in Ashland, Va. I'm not sure what I would have done if I didn't get in – I never thought it all the way through. For several months I entertained the idea of taking a year or two-long break after high school, moving to California, and to learning how to walk – I convinced myself I didn't want to graduate until I could do it on my feet. I finally realized I just needed to get college over with, though. The cost of living in California and distance from my family were also pretty big turn-offs. Big enough turn-offs to table the California thinking for a few more years.

> *Kristin decided about one month ago that if she didn't get into Randolph Macon, she would punt for one year and try again later. While I support her resolve, it was worrisome because sometimes momentum is needed to keep motivation constant. Well, we don't have to worry about that now...*
>
> *"Dad, guess what?! They called from Randolph Macon and I was accepted! Early admission! I don't have to worry about my grades in Trigonometry and Physics anymore!"*
>
> *I was elated for her, but quickly reminded her that she still has to graduate!*
>
> *"Sorry, kiddo, but you need to keep your grades up to make good on that acceptance. That's awesome that you got it done already! Now we can really focus on getting you ready."*
>
> *She was so excited. Hearing so much happiness in her voice was so refreshing.*

My blessing is, even though I decided against taking time off and I went to college after high school, I was still able to walk across the stage with a walker at my college graduation. But let's not jump ahead.

The first and most decisive characteristic of R-MC is its close proximity. A 20 minute drive could take me home for the weekend or Mom to meet me for lunch between classes, and that was very often the case. I'll admit it, I wasn't ready nor were my parents ready for me to be completely on my own when I was a freshman.

I thought I was, though. Along with the opportunity to test myself in living independently in a dorm room, I was excited for the chance to start over with a clean slate. I thought things would be different. I was throwing myself into a new group of people who didn't know me before my accident, my story, or seemingly every detail of my situation like my high school classmates were privileged to. I was excited to be surrounded by people who only knew me in one form: disabled. More than that, I was eager for the opportunity to be accepted as the person I am without a lingering memory of who I used to be. I thought making friends would be easy.

Before the end of the first few weeks, though, I saw how wrong I was. Academically speaking, Randolph-Macon is an outstanding institution full of well-qualified professors. Socially speaking, it is my nightmare.

My physical disability created an obstacle for my participation in events and attendance to parties; a majority of the buildings on campus are "historical" and therefore exempt from ADA regulation and equality for disabled students. That was the first challenge.

Making friends from in a wheelchair was yet another hill to climb. Again, my unique physical differences and struggles set me apart from kids my age. When I came to college, I thought friends would just happen naturally – I didn't think I would have to work so hard at it or put myself "out there" so much. That had never been the case for me before. In fact, I've never had a problem with making friends until I got to college.

For the first time in my life, I felt hopeless. So I spent that year alone.

Although it did lead to my alienation and countless weekends alone in my dorm room, not going to parties wasn't the worst case scenario. At the few I did attend at the even fewer accessible fraternity houses, the beer drips and drunken bodies that inevitably fell on my lap were hard to justify with their only mediocre entertainment. Unappealing as they were, those parties were also critical to the social life of Randolph-Macon, and my frat-party-absence resulted in me not meeting new people or making new friends. Like high school, college was my four-year-long struggle to fit in.

My first year in college is marked by a lot of my loneliness and a lot of my tears; it is one of the first times I remember being angry at God about my situation. I was angry with Him for my struggle and I was angry with Him for allowing me to have a disability that held me back from enjoying the "best years of my life." I felt alone.

Actually, besides my family, I was alone. The friends I did have were at other universities hours away, and my first years in college gave me no new ones. I felt hopeless in my situation and that's the biggest reason I spent as much time as I could off campus and away from it all.

In the few times I was in a non-academic social setting, I had an extremely hard time connecting with my peers. The burden of my wheelchair in an unfamiliar setting not only slights my self-confidence, it also acts as a social roadblock; an unfortunate majority of people feel uncomfortable addressing my unlikeliness, act differently around me, and/or take unnecessary pity on my situation. On top of that I didn't drink alcohol, do drugs, or have sex with strangers the way it seemed everyone else did. I just didn't fit in.

During my first year at R-MC, the few people I did interact with didn't take the time to be friends with me and didn't treat me the way I knew I deserved. My decision to not go to fraternity parties, whether because I couldn't get in or because I didn't want to get in, didn't help my situation at all. Attendance to these parties seemed to be my ticket into the social scene and, on a small campus with a small student body, my elusion was my social suicide. I missed my opportunity to make friends and for anybody to recognize me beyond seeing my wheelchair pushing down the sidewalks to class. At the rate of freshman year, "the girl in the wheelchair" is all I would ever be to anyone.

Many times I wondered if I just had to accept that's how it was going to be. Having a boyfriend? Forget it. Back when I was in high school I accepted that I would have to wait a long, long time until that was going to happen. Dating someone in a wheelchair is just too complicated and men my age just weren't mature enough – that's the excuse I'm using. Aside from the obvious hassle of accommodation, my wheelchair is somewhat of a stick in the mud when it comes to physical attraction. It's understandable, but still a heartbreak. No matter how many negotiations and pleads to God for someone to show interest in me, my dating life was stale as two month-old bread.

My liberation came at the beginning of my sophomore year and after nine months of confusion and heartache that made up my first year in college. In the summer before beginning sophomore year, I promised myself I was not going to live that over again. I promised myself that something had to change. I returned in September to no friends and uncomfortable surroundings, but I forced myself to go to the first meeting of Intervarsity, our on-campus Bible study group.

Immediately after the first Thursday night meeting, I began to find my happiness again. I was surrounded by people that were accepting, not judgmental of me, and had common interests. In the first month of attending weekly groups, I made friends that otherwise felt like an impossibility. I saturated myself in large group meetings, small group Bible studies, and all other events Intervarsity hosted around campus. The comfortable atmosphere and the addition of few, not many, friends into my life snapped me back into the outgoing person I had held in for so long.

Skipping forward to my junior and senior years, I had as many friends as I could count on two hands. Although not many, those people were all I needed to enjoy my college experience. I still had some nights alone in my room, but they came far less often and I even grew to enjoy them. My wheelchair still repelled all men, but I was okay with that for the time being.

When bad things happen that we can't immediately change, that's the only thing we can do: find beauty, force happiness.

I ended my years at Randolph-Macon College pretty well. Starting in sophomore year, I had a new attitude and a small but growing social group. Better yet, I wasn't living alone anymore. That was key, I think. The inclusion of one, eventually two, roommates into my apartment was my answer to the unhappiness I felt during my freshman year.

It took me a little bit longer than my peers, but I eventually got there – I eventually got comfortable with college life. At the end, the weekend was something I looked forward to instead of dreaded, and companionship was just half a mile and one phone call away. By the time graduation came, I was able to regret more than just leaving the environment of academia, but also leaving the friends that walked across the stage next to me.

This is the cool part of the story.

When graduation finally came around, it was my chance to fulfill another one of my dreams I had since being injured. First: survive. Second: graduate high school on time. Third: get accepted to college. And now: receive my college diploma. That diploma was symbolic of the end of my undergraduate studies, yes, but also of my success story. It was a reminder that I'm able to ride a rollercoaster of almost dying in the hospital, to trying to wiggle my toes in California, to getting accepted into college, then to graduating with a college degree. Even more, I wanted to graduate on my feet. I did it in high school and I wanted to do it again in college. That was the dream.

So that's what I worked for. I practiced with my leg braces and walker for what seemed like endless hours for the big day: graduation day. I wanted my gait to be perfect, my posture to be perfect, my speed to be perfect, everything to be perfect. Even more than I was showing off on stage to an audience of hundreds of people, I was proving to myself that I can do it. I was proving that I can be more than just paralyzed.

First at high school graduation and now at college, I was able to accomplish my 7-year-old dream of walking to accept my diploma. That was huge. In less than 7 years I went from lying on a hospital bed with doctors telling me I will never walk again, to walking on my feet to accept a degree.

I remember standing in the middle of the stage and looking into the crowd of clapping people. I was absolutely on top of the world. In that moment, everything was worth it.

College was a hard time for me. My first years were filled with desolation and grief, and my last years were filled with relative happiness and ease. Logistically speaking, my life post-injury requires extra effort for me to settle into and feel comfortable in new environments. As result,

I miss out on some initial friendships and engagements with people around me, often leading to my solitude. That defines my first year in college. The only reason I've been able to avoid a complete depression is, as corny as it sounds, to surround myself with positivity and trust that better days are coming.

I know – easier said than done.

My disability is responsible for giving a purpose to my life, a goal for me to work toward, and a mature perspective. As consequence, I missed out on the carefree and usually reckless experiences that are expected at my young age. But it was a good trade. The memories that came out of my time in college are bumpy at first but, like most other things in a life of disability, got better with a lot of waiting, a lot of effort, and a lot of prayer.

Thank God it's over, though.

Saturday, May 26 (6 years & 9 months after injury)
– An entry from Dad's CaringBridge journal

Today is May 26 and it's beautiful outside at the "Center of the Universe" – Ashland, Virginia. My family is all together. I take a deep breath and thank God that I am here to see Kristin graduate from college. As I sit outside and look at all the families gathered here to watch as their children start another chapter in their lives, I am nervous, but also on the verge of yet another flood of emotion. I can feel it coming. Deep breath. It will be OK, it will be OK.

Earlier that day...

"So, Kristin, what did you do last night? Hang out with friends? Go to a party? Stay up late?"

"Well I went out with my friends for a little while, but I came home early to practice."

Kristin decided she was going to walk across the stage to receive her diploma. This meant she would need to use her braces, a walker, coordinate the timing so as not to disrupt the ceremony, etc.

A friend told me long ago, "Make sure she gets her college education. She's got so many challenges; she will need that diploma to help pull her through." I have never forgotten those words. There have definitely been some challenging semesters along the way. On top of physical challenges, Kristin suffered a traumatic brain injury, which seriously affected her short term memory. Imagine going through college with that struggle. It easily takes twice as much effort.

But back to the ceremony...

As we watched with anticipation, Rhonda and I never said it, but we were both thinking, "What if she falls? What if her walk is viewed by everyone as a prolonged interruption? That would break her heart; this is so important to her."

The rock of our family since the accident, Kristin's best friend and sister, Jessica, will be helping Kristin on stage by moving her wheelchair from one side to the other after The Walk.

"Kristin Elizabeth Beale..."

As Kristin rose from her wheelchair from the side of the stage, her leg braces were visible for only a second. She stood up and held on to her walker. It was in slow motion as she turned and made her way step by step towards the President of Randolph Macon College. Almost immediately, the entire crowd of families, students and faculty rose to their feet with a standing ovation. They continued to clap from the time she stood up, during The Walk and until she sat back down in her chair at the other end of the stage. From somewhere behind me, I heard, "THAT IS AWESOME" amidst the applause.

Before she wheeled off the stage with her diploma in her hand, she gave a fist pump to the crowd. Another deep breath, but this time to choke back the tears. Kristin closes the chapter on yet another accomplishment.

Just a few years ago, we watched and prayed that she would simply survive a horrific event. Little by little, our hearts have been broken as we watched friendships dissolve, physical challenges become serious problems, frustrations run high, and faith be tested. Time after time, God has guided Kristin and us along the way. We have learned to breathe deep more often than not.

Today, we watched as the human spirit and faithful heart defeat yet another attempt by negativity, discourse and apathy to hold Kristin back from moving forward. Today, we took another deep breath.

CHAPTER 20

New York

My handcycling career started in January while I was lying in
bed looking through a Facebook album of a friend I know
from college.

Like myself, he's dependent on a wheelchair but, unlike myself at the
time, is also very involved in adaptive sports. The album I was looking
through was him in the New York Marathon riding in a funny looking

bike he pedaled with his arms. His pictures looked like fun and I was bored, so I wandered around the internet to find out more about it.

One thing led to another and I ended up on the website of the Christopher and Dana Reeve Foundation. From there I read about Team Reeve, and from there I learned about Achilles International. The mission statement displayed at the top of their site is what drew me in:

> *"...to enable people with all types of disabilities to participate in mainstream athletics in order to promote personal achievement, enhance self-esteem, and lower barriers to living a fulfilling life."*

And they had my full attention. I clicked on links, read a couple of short articles, and decided I wanted to be part of the team.

In moments of impulse, I registered myself for both Team Reeve and Achilles International. Once I was a member of Achilles, a few clicks later I was signed up to participate in the New York City Marathon in November of the same year.

Special attention to the word "impulse."

I was very sleepy and it's still kind of a blur in my memory. I didn't know how many miles make up a marathon or, honestly, anything else about it. But it can't be that big of a deal, right?

A few months passed and it was July and I had 100% forgotten about handcycling, Achilles International, and everything did so late at night and so many months ago. To be honest, the fact that I didn't tell anyone about it makes me think I forgot everything by the next morning when I woke up. Try to imagine my surprise when a representative from Achilles International called me at the end of the month to introduce herself and see how my training was going. She talked about the events leading up to the marathon, logistics of the weekend, and other members of Achilles she was in contact with.

"How many miles long is a marathon? What is the hand-bike called? Is it hard?"

Those were questions I wanted to ask her, but decided to play it cool to hide my shock and potential embarrassment. I casually [or that's what I tried to make it seem] told her I hadn't been training because I didn't own a bike.

I don't remember her reaction, but I imagine it was laced with surprise and maybe a little bit of urgency. She said I could borrow a handcycle (the official word for "hand-bike") from Achilles and use the remaining 4 months to train as much as possible. It was ridiculous and maybe even a bad decision on my part, but I was determined to do that marathon and no one dared stand in my way.

Fast forward some months. I received a handcycle from Achilles International to train for the New York Marathon, and it sat in my garage collecting dust. My excuses for not training were easy to retrieve: it was too cold, I had things to do, I didn't feel like it, the list goes on. In complete honesty, I just forgot. While I had every intention of completing the marathon, it still felt like a dream.

In my defense, though, I did go out riding a couple of times around our small neighborhood. In the end my "training" lasted 2, maybe 3 hours total. It's an understatement to say that I was not ready to do a marathon and this was absolutely another [eventually comical] example of my impulsive recklessness.

My doctor seemed to agree with the former; he strongly recommended against my participation with little-to-no training. I wasn't surprised and was ready to ignore his advice, but he started talking about my rotator cuff, damage leading to surgery, and all the terrible things. I can't remember if this scared me out of doing the marathon or scared my parents out of letting me do the marathon, but I was not going to do the marathon. My New York Marathon dreams were put on hold.

Crushed…the only other dream Kristin has had since being able to walk across the stage to get her high school diploma was to do the NYC marathon. To be taken out by this news virtually sucked the life from her. Simply put, she was crushed.

The marathon came and went, the year came and went, and the warm weather came and went. When I went on a handcycling-hiatus the previous year, I told myself I would train and be ready to ride New York the next year – but that also came and went. I cycled through my excuses until I finally forgot about it altogether and didn't snap out of it until, again, I was contacted by Achilles International.

Like the previous year, I received a phone call in late July to inquire about my participation in the marathon and, true to form, I enthusiastically agreed. Only slightly improved from the previous year, I rode my bike for a total of about 3 hours before my enthusiasm faded and my bike returned to its spot in the corner of the garage. I decided not to consult my doctor, and instead develop a foundationless overconfidence that I would finish a marathon, training or not. I'm not sure where that confidence came from but I was going with it. "Headstrong" is a good adjective to use here.

With reason, my parents were nervous wrecks throughout this whole process. They had the doctor's warnings in their heads and knowledge of my meager attempts at preparation, and stood firmly opposed to my dreams of the marathon. The only thing that made them change their minds was the optional "guides" Achilles International provides for their athletes – basically just two new friends to run alongside me and help if and when help is needed. I had previously turned down the offer due to my overconfidence, but having them there sealed the deal with my parents, so I let it happen.

The next day I called Achilles International, announced my turnaround decision on marathon guides, and was matched with two names: Maryann and Josh. That decision and those people are what made the New York Marathon one of the most awesome and prideful experiences of my life. It was also the beginning of one of the best friendships of my life.

In every way, my accident broke me. I went from being the captain of my lacrosse team, field hockey team player, and a 9-year competition cheerleader, to lying in a hospital bed unable to open my right eye. Adaptive sports after my injury have given me the chance to prove to myself and everyone else that my body is still able.

I have tried every adaptive sport available to me and handcycling is by far my favorite. In fact, it has meant more to me than I ever could have imagined. I'm the happiest when I'm riding my bike. Although it's still a piece of equipment that's unfamiliar to most people, it doesn't shout "DISABILITY" in the way my wheelchair does. My bike brings me closer to normalcy and is not as distinctly off-putting as a wheelchair. To be in the world using something that intrigues people to ask questions and be open minded versus jump to conclusions and stereotypes in their minds, is surprisingly relieving.

My handcycle also gives me the opportunity to physically work hard and see the results of my effort reflected in my time, distance, and/or muscle definition. My life post-injury has been filled with ambiguity and blurry lines in terms of my body, and riding my bike is one of the few certainties I have. Riding my handcycle and participation in marathons has not only given me a tangible goal to work toward, it also gives me something people can feel impressed with, instead of feeling pity for my situation.

The New York Marathon was the beginning of my marathon career, but it was also the beginning of one of the most fulfilling activities of my adult life. With my handcycle, I found a joy that was otherwise unknown.

In a very large way, my ability to stay active and involved in sports has been the calming force in my post-paralyzed life. When my mind and efforts are focused on playing a sport, I feel as close to an able-bodied Kristin than I do in any other activity. Sports allow me to distract from the constant humming of my body, the never-ending stress of merging myself into an able-bodied world, and all the interpersonal repercussions of my situation. Sports give me the chance to back-seat the bug bites that a paralyzed adulthood brings.

Adaptive sports have given me an outlet, an intention, and my sanity. With handcycling, though, I have found my happiness.

I realize I haven't said anything about the actual marathon yet. Did I finish? Did I hurt myself? How long did it take me? I won't answer the last question, but I will say that I didn't hurt myself. And I finished, which was a medium-sized miracle.

She did it.

I could go on for pages about this past weekend. There weren't many dry eyes in the Beale family. Kristin's hardcore determination won out again as she crossed the finish line in the NYC Marathon in a handcycle and received her medal.

But let's not skip ahead. Despite 26.2 being the most intimidating number of miles and a marathon requiring more effort to run/handcycle than most normal people are willing to put toward any one thing, I had fun. I had so, so much fun.

We went to the 7 mile mark to wait for Kristin's arrival. The lump in my throat got even bigger as I watched her coming up the street pumping her arms as hard as she could with a huge smile on her face. As she described it later, "I felt so free." She was moving fast and in control – loving every stroke on that bike. She took a brief water break and Rhonda immediately started piddling, adjusting, and hovering. It looked like a Beale pit crew. Very funny.

"Dad I feel GREAT. I'm having so much fun." Josh and Maryann gave me the real reports, which were all very positive. They, too, were smiling. I truly believe they were having as much fun as Kristin, trying to keep up with her.

Although we had a "race tracker" on my phone, it was very hard to find Kristin during the race. At one point, I saw Josh and Maryann around the 24th mile.

"Where's Kristin?"

As they ran by, they shouted back, "She blew past us! She's up there somewhere!"

I had to laugh. She left the guides. That's my girl.

Again, I could go on for a while here. Suffice to say, Kristin has added yet another accomplishment to her list: snow skiing, lacrosse, surfing, and now a marathon. She's a rock star.

CHAPTER 21

Achilles Jones

S ome people say you can't buy your friends, but I wholeheartedly disagree; I bought my best friend from the internet for $250. People also say a dog is a man's best friend, and it took me owning my own dog to realize how true that is. I am not a man, but my dog is my best friend and her name is Achilles Jones.

Less than one month after graduating college, I started researching puppies. I had just moved from living in a college dorm room with 2 friends and a never-ending stream of visitors, all my friends at my fingertips, and a social opportunity at any time of the day, to a house in the suburbs with my parents. Needless to say, the transition after graduation was a big one. I'm not saying it wasn't a happy one or that it's not exactly where I wanted to be – I'm just saying that I needed a puppy.

I crowded the Favorites list on my computer with links to Boston Terriers, English Bulldogs, Dachshunds, Pomeranians, and what seemed like every other breed of small dog I could find. I spent countless hours researching dog care, expenses, benefits, and logistics, and tabulated my information into a PowerPoint presentation for my parents. I served dinner, dressed fancy, and introduced my idea in the most business-like way I could.

Mom and Dad listened to my proposition, considered the possibility, and washed away my efforts with one strong, incisive counterargument: Mom will end up taking care of the dog and it'll become a family dog, as opposed to only my dog. That thought was unappealing enough for me to closet my puppy dreams and move on to another animal.

My next venture was a monkey. They live in cages, poop in diapers, ride on shoulders, and fit into pockets. A monkey is an ideal pet for me and I had to make my parents see that. I did research for one week, put together another PowerPoint, and presented it to them in the same fashion. My plan seemed foolproof until Dad brought up two deal-breaking points: there's nowhere to board a monkey when I go out of town and I'll have trouble finding an apartment complex that allows monkey roommates. I agreed and moved on to another animal.

During the next months I researched, made a PowerPoint for, and pleaded with my parents to own a turtle, snake, fox, sugar glider, salt water fish, and hedgehog. Like before, Dad thought of all the annoying [and usually legitimate] reasons each pet is not good for me, and emphasized each of them to the tune of my breaking heart. Mom and Dad both agreed that maintaining a pet cage is my biggest challenge, with evidence from my five childhood hamsters who spent their short existence in insufferably foul smelling and poop-infested habitats. I agreed and moved on to a more suitable and less constricted animal: teacup pig.

Again, I found the ideal pet. Maturing to 12-25lbs and standing only 11-14 inches high, teacup pigs claim to be minimal hassle for maximum satisfaction. They poop in a litter box, require moderate exercise, eat pellets of food, and easily adapt to apartment life. So I slid into a two-month-long infatuation. Pigs were occupying my thoughts, intentions, and interactions with anyone and everyone who stood still long enough to listen to me talk. I drove my parents crazy by way of three PowerPoint presentations, a myriad of quoted testimonials, and countless conversations. Despite my efforts and sleepless nights of research, they just wouldn't accept the idea of cohabitation with a pig.

As if it was my plan all along, my persistence of a pet piglet made my previous animal undertakings more appealing to my parents. One night at the conclusion of a heated discussion at the dinner table, Mom gave me an ultimatum.

"Kristin," she said so seriously. "If you stop talking about pigs we'll let you get a puppy."

"I don't want a puppy," I immediately pushed back. "A pig is better."

A dog was so far from my mind at this point and it was hard to switch gears; I had been set on a pig for so long that even a puppy was unappealing. My parents argued that owning a dog is easier, more loveable, and more practical than a teacup pig or any of the other animals I found.

All it took was five minutes of discussion and my running imagination to 100% flip back to the possibility of a puppy. With their approval and a browser full of bookmarks, I was set on fire. I was getting a puppy.

I revisited the websites still saved in my Favorites, added new ones, and spent every available minute of my free time looking at dogs on the internet. I researched breed-related health issues, weighed the options of big versus small dogs, evaluated quality of breeders, and considered every component of finding the perfect companion. Narrowing my dog search down seemed like a never-ending process, but I finally reasoned that time spent searching for a dog was delaying time spent actually owning a dog. I had to make a decision.

I went back to the website of a brown, female Pomapoo puppy and decided she had to be my final search. I deleted all other dogs from my archive and never turned back. She was located within driving distance, cost $250, and had updated shots. At a mere 3 months old, my daughter weighed only 3.5lbs.

By the time I set my mind on the Pomapoo, I was at the end of a long deliberation for a name. With the help of my family and some friends, I repeated the process of giving her a name, changing my mind, and renaming her about 100 times. When she came to me on November 14, I wavered for still another two weeks before I decided on the name Achilles.

Along with being a hero in Greek mythology, Achilles is significant to me in a big way. Achilles International is the offspring of the Christopher and Dana Reeve Foundation and is responsible for my opportunity to participate in the New York Marathon and an ongoing list that makes up my marathon career. They have given me an invaluable privilege of not only using a handcycle, but the ability to fill a gap that sports occupied when I was an able-bodied teenager. Being a member of a sports team has meant a lot to me and membership with Achilles International has been an answered prayer. All that considered, Achilles was the obvious choice of a name for my daughter.

The middle name "Jones" was a beautiful accident. In the days of no bladder control and a weak sphincter muscle, Achilles was leaving puddles and piles in all corners and open areas of the house. One Saturday when my parents were at the river and we were home alone, I discovered an Achilles poop in the dining room and chased her around the house as punishment. Imagine me in my wheelchair chasing around this tiny, 3 pound fleck of a puppy. In hindsight, it's pretty funny.

In the heat of the moment and with no premeditation, I yelled at "Achilles Jones" instead of just "Achilles." I laughed as soon as it came out of my mouth and decided Jones will be her middle name. It took a time of acclimation for everyone, but she eventually learned to respond to "Achilles," "Achilles Jones," "Jones," and even "Joe."

Kristin continues to "shock and awe" us with her insight and spirit. Every week, she says something that makes us think deeper and appreciate life more. As you know, her determination already resulted in a dog, which she named Achilles in honor of her marathon team, Achilles International. For some reason, which is still being debated, she added Jones to the name. Her name is now Achilles Jones. It's just funny. The whole family has taken it to the next level, as we are known for doing. If Achilles goes to the river, she's automatically "River Jones," or is eating a bone, it's a "Jones Bone," etc. The best part is when she comes to greet Rhonda at the door, she's a "Grandmama Jones" or "Dumping Kristin Jones."

Achilles has destroyed carpets, shoes, and furniture, but has won the hearts of everyone. Cody and Chloe, our family dogs, may feel differently. They are tortured by Achilles – the energizer bunny of dogs. The older I get, the less I care about "stuff". We can't take it with us, folks.

Adopting Achilles has been the best decision I've made in my life. Even during the frustrating months it took to house-break her, I have loved her every minute and with every part of myself. She is someone that is always happy to be around me and is there when people consistently and inevitably disappoint. In regards to friends and boyfriends, the lack of companionship in my life has been overwhelming. Achilles makes me feel appreciated and wanted in a way humans have not.

People say you can't buy your friends, but I wholeheartedly disagree. I bought my best and smallest friend from the internet for $250, and her name is Achilles Jones.

CHAPTER 22

Marine Corps

"If you look to the sky," a man announced on the loudspeaker, "there is a 7,800 square foot American flag falling from a helicopter. Marine and Army veterans will jump out of them holding flags from every military division."

In my experience, the production at the start line of the Marine Corps Marathon has always been a well-planned and extremely patriotic event: a choir sings the National Anthem, a cannon is fired, and American flags can be seen in all directions. I looked to the sky at the production of falling men and felt pride unlike I had felt since the opening ceremony last year. My eyes filled with water of happiness as I watched the falling veterans. My body was swallowed by an overwhelming comfort and conviction for the hours ahead of me.

As soon as the flag descended to the ground and the choir finished singing, I looked beside me at Mom smiling and bouncing up and down with the rhythm of Cotton Eyed Joe on the loudspeaker. She was waving her arms at her sides in a pattern that reminded me of Achilles Jones when I smush my hands around her face.

"Are you ready?" she asked energetically. "We have fifty more minutes until you take off."

Her body was still bouncing to the music, bouncing.

I shook my head up and down and smiled. Despite three layers of sleeves and thick mittens, my arms were getting cold and my fingers becoming numb. My body was becoming frigid and distraction is the only thing I could do to preserve my marathon-body. I repeated a prayer I had been reciting in my head all morning, asking God to not let me hurt my rotator cuffs, wrists, or deltoid muscles. I filled my head with as many things as I could to not think about the outside temperature or remaining wait time. Somehow we got through it, though. Thank God that Mom was there with me.

I pulled my cell phone from the fanny pack around my waist and saw a text message from Josh, my marathon buddy. Last year was our first marathon together (New York) and this year he was sending me encouragement all the way from Boston.

"ARE YOU READY?" Josh texted. His text was in all capital letters, which drew my enthusiasm up one more level. I responded ("I'M READY" then a trail of marathon-relevant emojis). It was cool to have Josh there with me, if only in spirit. I put my phone back in my fanny and turned my focus back on the road ahead of me.

"One minute until handcycle start," the announcer's voice finally echoed in my head after 49 minutes of shivering and bouncing. Mom looked at me, nodded, and slinked away to leave me sitting alone at the start line. I repositioned my race number – 588 – to be visible on my chest, and waited for the countdown.

My body started buzzing and the hum from the bodies around me got louder. I sat in my bike and in position behind the line, and felt alien to my surroundings while I listened to the 30 second countdown conclude. Before I anticipated and maybe before I was ready, a cannon fired to my right and the crowd gave a powerful cheer. Followed by 120 disabled athletes, I raced through and past all the people and onto mile one of twenty six.

During the week leading up to the Marine Corps Marathon, I set a goal for myself to stay ahead of the runners and handcyclers during the race. Despite the first 3 miles of the race sitting on an incline, I was determined to stay ahead.

Too soon, the handcycles caught up and I had to revise my goal to center around my experience rather than my performance; my lack of training set me back more than I thought it would and I was better to strive for a fun time instead of a decreased time.

Inside the first 2 miles, the able-bodied runners came from my background to my foreground, and I was surrounded. I fought those uphill miles as hard as I could and until my arms felt like they were going to pop off. Meanwhile, able-bodies ran past me with apparent ease.

"It's okay," I thought with a stroke of bitterness as my vision filled with tight athlete butts. "I'll catch you all on the downhill."

The miles grew long and I was consumed by runners from all sides. My struggle was not as much of a secret as I tried to keep it, either. What seemed like every runner who ran past me went out of their way to say encouraging things: "you're doing great, Wheels," "keep pushing, 588," "you're almost to the top, girl."

It was amazing. Instead of saving their strength to run the many miles still ahead of us, people were using their energy to say things to and motivate me. One time I even received a "good job, young man." Ouch.

Encouragement from other runners didn't always make me speed up, but it definitely made me feel like I wasn't alone in my struggle.

In those first moments of pushing up the hill I could force out a rare "thank you" and sometimes a weak smile to runners who spoke; it took too much effort to use my facial muscles and I couldn't find my voice. When I made it to the downhill, though, that was a different story. I was looking both runners and fans in the eyes, smiling with all my teeth, and responding with "thank you" and "you too" to nearly everyone who spoke to me. Some responded with a smile, but mostly I talked to their butts as they ran past.

Another beautiful surprise was the amount of people who stepped up to help clear a path within the runners for my handcycle to ride through. The responsibility started with a middle-aged black man, then passed to a young man in a kilt, then passed to a woman in purple tie-dye, and continued a stream of runners clearing my path like it was their job. Without my asking, they ran ahead of me and screamed at the dense crowd of people to "make a hole" or "move to the right" so I could get through. When one person's energy drained and they fell behind, another person would step in within the same minute to continue the job. Sometimes I tried to contribute, but my voice is as loud as a worm and I wasn't heard by anyone.

The attention being drawn to my "wheels on the left" or "bike behind" caused other runners to notice me and keep up the encouragement. More than a couple of times, a group of 10 or more runners in my vicinity started clapping and shouting words like "good job, babe," or "push through it." The camaraderie between these runners was incredible. Also they called me "babe" so that was exciting.

My favorite encouragements came from the runners behind me who tried to say something, but the effort from running made their words a whisper. A few times and always unexpectedly, I heard the soft tune of "keep going, baby" or "you're so close" in my ear. The whispers it made me laugh and again, my struggle didn't seem so heavy.

The other part of the marathon-atmosphere is the fans on the sidelines. There are so many people lined up to cheer on the runners; the Marine Corps Marathon is the third largest marathon in the U.S.

and the eighth in the world for spectator attendance and recognition. Overflowing past the orange cones, people were holding up signs with phrases that read "Toenails Are Overrated," "Your Feet Hurt Because You're Kicking Ass," and "Run for Free Beer." As I passed by they screamed "way to go, 588," "go Team Achilles," and similar phrases that made me feel equally as awesome. Everyone around me had the Marathon Spirit and it was hard not to catch it.

As I rounded a corner at the Lincoln Memorial, I saw Jessica bouncing up and down on the sidelines. She was surrounded by people on all sides, but somehow I spotted her immediately. She was screaming cheers at me and holding up a banner that said "TEAM KRISTIN." Beside her, Mom was waving her hand at high speeds and Dad was holding a sign that said "HOT WHEELS" with an illustration of [handcycle] tires with flames coming from behind them. It was obviously Jessica's work. I wanted to stop and smile at them, but I had to keep going. With a humongous smile on my face, I sped on.

By the time I reached mile 18, all course-clearing assistance from the other runners had either fallen back or run ahead of me, and my enthusiasm was starting to wear off. I was able to weave through the crowd by myself and felt more alone with every person I passed. I searched my mind for distractions from the pain of my upper body as the hills kept getting steeper, the day hotter, and my vision drunker. I filled my mouth with energy gels not because I needed a sugar boost, but because they gave me a taste that made me feel happy, if only until I swallowed. I searched my head for motivation and cycled through Team Achilles, Josh, and the finisher's medal, but nothing lasted. My mind was blank as I pushed down the road to the finish line.

Mile 21 was where I found the best surprise of the whole marathon: donut holes. With the intention of grabbing a cup of Gatorade from a drink station, I slowed down to a group of college-aged men holding paper cups on the side of the road.

"Donut?" he asked me with an eager and hurried voice. In a body that was foreign, I felt my head nodding up and down and a smile spread across my face. Our encounter only lasted a couple of seconds: I nodded, he threw a cup toward me filled with two large donut holes, and I coasted past. I was surprised and jubilant as I crammed them in my mouth and savored the prize I hadn't deserved for 9 long years. They were remarkable and worth every gram of sugar. With a fresh streak of donut-hole-energy, I pushed on.

Completing mile 26 means I was near the finish line and, with that realization, my whole mind filled with dread. The Marine Corps Marathon is infamous for its final uphill challenge; the last .2 of the 26.2 mile long race is well-known for being the most demanding and painful because of the 45 degree slope to the finish line. The end of this marathon and I have a love/hate relationship. I gathered as much momentum as possible from the downhill and chugged my bike toward the finish.

After about 50 yards, all of my downhill-momentum was gone and replaced by the spirit of people bending over and shouting confidence in my ear. I heard a familiar voice in the commotion and looked to my left to see Jessica, Mom, and Dad running behind the spectators and yelling my name. Jessica was holding the "Team Kristin" banner high in the air. My arms gave a weak flicker of energy and I pushed my bike two inches closer to the top.

At the steepest part of the hill I turned my head barely in time to stop anyone from seeing an uncontrollable and hugely unattractive weep spread across my face. My fatigued body doesn't know any other reaction to my strain than to contort and cry. At this point in my marathon career, my finish-line-ugly-cry is calculable and relatively easy to hide. My body was exhausted, arms sore, and the finish line is barely within my reach.

With my head still facing away from the crowd, I switched my bike into its lowest gear and crawled up the hill as slow as a slug.

I reached the top after what seemed like 30 minutes, but was probably only 2. My bike floated down the 50 yards of flat road to the finish line and my vision was blurred. Whether the blur was from my strain or from my weird crying routine, I'm not sure.

I merged my bike into a line of Marines waiting to put medals around the necks of marathon finishers. The most memorable part of the Marine Corps Marathon is the constant presence of Marines handing out Gatorade, cheering from the sidelines, and, best of all, awarding medals to finishers. I was eager to see the long-hidden medal design, and rolled to the closest and most attractive Marine I could spot.

"Congratulations," he said and forced a medal over my helmet and around my neck.

I weak smiled and looked down for one instant to admire my prize before moving forward with the crowd. Another Marine jumped out to give me a plastic bag, and another guided me through a line to receive a banana, water bottle, and snack box. My actions felt numb and my surroundings were still blurry as I drifted through the crowd of tired athletes. My bike coasted down the line, I grabbed my last freebie [a bottle of Recovery Gatorade] and parked my bike near a grass area to process and to breathe for the first time since finishing the race.

My family ran to me minutes later, sang accolades, and gave hugs to my limp and fatigued body. Aside from a post-marathon banana, reuniting and seeing their support is the best thing. I sat for another minute and listened to their bubble before Jessica grabbed the back of my handcycle seat and guided it me the Achilles International Meeting Room.

Still floating, I collected my wheelchair, said goodbye to new friends from the weekend, and climbed into Dad's truck for our two hour trip home. I felt like a spectator watching another person's life; my body was just going through the motions.

Kristin successfully completed the Marine Corps Marathon. The MCM was only her second and she's already hooked. It's all I can do to keep her from wanting to do one in Canada next. As you would imagine, the sight of her working her way through the 26.2 miles was inspirational, but to answer your question (and hers), NO, I'm not even tempted to do one with her. It was a great event in that Jessica came home and we were there as a family supporting every stroke of that bike.

The moments during a marathon that I'm in the most pain and that seem the most impossible are the times I feel the happiest. I can't think about or understand it until the race is over, but the perfect happiness that fills me up in these moments is indescribable. There's a joy that flows in my spirit when I'm using all of my mental, emotional, and physical effort to reach a goal. Achilles International has been my greatest link to the world of athletics I lost in my accident, and my greatest source of happiness since I was paralyzed in 2005.

CHAPTER 23

The Shamrock

"I think you're supposed to roll to the white line," Dad said. His voice snapped me out of the daze my mind was stuck in. "That's what they're doing."

"Yes," I responded and saw two other handcyclers zoned out next to me. We were at the start line a full 30 minutes before the race started and it was completely unnecessary to move forward another two feet. A tiny man stood on a tiny stage under an inflatable canopy next to the start line and scream-talked at the shivering crowd through a microphone. I was perfectly happy to be sitting at a distance, but Dad was stressing about it so I might as well appease him. With shaking hands and a jacket covering almost my entire face, I pushed my bike forward to the start.

My hands were shaking because of the cold. Maybe St. Patrick's Day used to bring warm weather, but in my memory it has always been bitter cold. For some logical reasons, marathon season is also during that cold time of the year. Dad and I were standing at the starting line of the Shamrock Marathon in Virginia Beach, shaking. My arms were shaking, teeth chattering, and fingertips turning white, but I was ready. I hadn't hardly trained on my handcycle since the Marine Corps Marathon four months prior, but I was feeling all right about it. I felt ready.

> *True to form, Kristin trained about 4 times before this race. We woke up early on Sunday morning to be at the start by 7:30. It was cold. No, wait – it was frigid. The high for the day was predicted at 40 degrees with 19 mph wind gusts, making it feel like 35 degrees. And, of course, the race primarily takes place on the oceanfront. Why people want to do a marathon in this weather is beyond me. Kristin, I assure you, wants this.*

"30 seconds until handcycle start," I heard the tiny man's voice boom over the loud speaker.

"Okay," Dad looked down to me and said. "I love you, sweetie. See you at the finish line."

I nodded my head pointedly and focused my eyes to the course ahead of me. If I wasn't going to train for this marathon, I had to bring all of my mental awareness to my body. There's a fine line between pain I can push through and pain I have to attend to, and it takes my full awareness to discern. I spent the last minutes before I started on the 26.2 mile journey switching from Morning Mode to Marathon Mode.

"Countdown to start," I heard the tiny man say again. I looked to my left and saw Dad smiling at me by the canopy. "10...9...8..."

I looked over to my right at the handcyclers sitting next to me and felt a connection with them. We were going to take on this challenge together, at the front of the crowd, ahead of all other runners. Together.

"3…2…1," I heard the tiny man screaming again – before I was ready. A horn blew and my handcycling friends zoomed ahead of me. I never saw them again. Of course I took that personally.

Despite her lack of training, Kristin took off as the very first one to cross the start line with a huge frozen smile on her face. I've never been able to block the hitch in my breath and the water in my eyes as I see her move forward with so much real happiness on her face. I think most parents understand when they see their children accomplish something.

Very soon and despite my miniscule head start, the runners caught up to me on the course. At first only a few men ran past me, but it wasn't long and until strangers were coming up from all sides. Even though it meant I was no longer at the head of the pack, I much preferred the company of other runners. It gets lonely.

"How about I tie a rope to you and ride along," I heard a man's voice yell to me aggressively. I looked to my left and saw him running beside me, looking at me sideways, and grinning like he made a quality joke.

"Yeah," I yelled back at him with a big, fake smile. "Hop on when we get to a downhill."

He cascaded into laughter and kept up his pace. My comeback was equally as unfunny, but I was adapting to my audience. To avoid any additional dialogue with this man, I pushed hard and rode in front of him.

The first 5 miles of the marathon seemed to last forever. I saw a mile-marking flag in the distance and expected it to indicate at least mile 8, but it only said mile 4. I was surrounded by the butts of every kind of runner: some who looked weightless and floating across the road; some who stumbled over their own feet; and others who looked like they were just going through the motions, not fully aware of their surroundings. One man ran ahead of me and shot the most impressive snot rocket I've ever seen. I thought about and replayed the scene of his rocket in my head for miles after. I don't think I'll ever forget it.

There are two things that make participation in marathons my favorite thing to do: the free swag (t-shirts, bags, and most importantly the medal) and the energy gummies. The miles before the 13.1 halfway point are usually the most difficult, and having a Ziploc bag full of fruit-flavored gummy happiness in my fanny pack is a comfort for me. I'm not sure whether the effects of the gummies are immediate or my beliefs about their effectiveness is immediate, but the same second I put one in my mouth a streak of power shoots through my fingertips. At mile 7, I visited the Ziploc in my fanny pack. At mile 7, things got serious.

The cold weather brings not only hazard of my upper body freezing and shaking to death, but also the hazard of my fingers freezing and snapping off. My solution is thin, black gloves with tiny, rubber balls on the palms. The only negative about my gloves is they make it nearly impossible to dig through my fanny, into my Ziploc, and to my gummies. I have to eat the gummies in clumps of 3 or more.

One time I made the mistake of putting a 3-gummy-clump in my mouth while I rode through a heavily fan-populated area. I tried to smile at them in thanks for cheering, and three multi-colored, vomit-resembling gum-blobs fell from my lips and onto the course. There's an art I quickly learned of energy-gummy-consumption during a marathon: do it alone.

"Good job, girl in the pink helmet," a voice came from behind. I looked around and saw a man run past me with one thumb in the air. Usually people call me "Wheelchair," Achilles," or "Wheels," but "Girl in the Pink Helmet" was a new one. It was specific enough that I think he might have planned out the comment then waited for the perfect moment to say it within my earshot. That's why I love my marathon family.

I pushed my handcycle down the course and through the constant, never-boring crowds for another 2 hours until I finally reached mile

13 and I was finally halfway done. Ironically, halfway through the marathon is when the struggle starts to get easier.

"Okay," I whispered under my breath. "Another one of those then I'm done. I can do this."

It's not that I was looking forward to the end of the marathon, because that's not the case at all. The truth is, my motivation is rooted in the finisher's medal and the finisher's banana. A medal and gummies are the best things about participating in a marathon, but a medal and a banana are the best things about completing a marathon.

At miles 15-18, the course led me on a long, straight road surrounded by trees. The road was flat and smooth, and my bike glided over it with ease. There was a crowd of people running at my left and one particularly attractive man running at my right.

"How long have you been riding?" he shouted to me. I pushed extra hard to reach him, then slowed down a little bit to remain next to him. I am very sneaky.

Even considering my premeditation, I was so surprised and excited by his dialogue. Even though we were 2/3 of the way into a marathon and he was sweating through his hair and clothes, his voice was even and gentle. He was like an angel.

"For 3 years," I responded. I softened my lips and tried to match his temper. "New York Marathon."

"That's really cool," he said. Our conversation was casual. We talked like we were sitting in my living room, not on mile 18 of the Shamrock Marathon. "Where are you from?"

"Richmond," I said. He was very good looking and was talking to me, so I tried to be cool. I was feeling good about myself. "How about you?"

"South Carolina," he said. "Columbia. I went to school there but I'm originally from Missouri."

"What did you go to school for?" I asked. A marathon is no time for small talk, but I was going with it.

"I got my degree in Business," he told me. "What about you? And where did you go?"

"I went to Randolph-Macon in Virginia," I said. "I got my degree in Clinical Psychology."

"Cool," he smiled. We were still in a living room. "I like living in South Carolina. The weather is warm."

"My parents have a house in Florida and I like the weather there too," I offered. "It's so much warmer than Virginia."

"Yeah," he said. "The weather in South Carolina is warm sometimes too."

We talked about the weather, the lamest of conversation topics, for another 30 seconds before we caught up to another crowd of people. I fell behind him to pass through a hole in the middle of the group. We were a cute couple.

When we were free on the other side, though, he kept running and didn't look back or try to catch me again. I was disappointed, to say the least. I thought I had at least made a new Facebook friend, but I guess not. I never saw him again.

My next source of entertainment were the signs that stuck in the grass along the course. Some had weird, wannabe-inspirational quotes ("May the sun shine all day long, everything go right, nothing wrong"), some had jokes ("Why don't you iron 4-leaf-clovers? You don't want to press your luck."), and some were just confusing ("What do you call a leprechaun that falls in the lake? A wet leprechaun"). Lame as they were, they helped pass the time and pass the miles. I was thankful for every sign that lined the long, otherwise straight and boring road through the woods. They distracted me from my efforts, if nothing else.

The last miles of the marathon passed fairly quickly. After I reached mile 18, the end felt close enough to energize me through the final distance. The course followed a flat, long road that led to nowhere. I pushed the handles of my handcycle as hard as my body would allow, then noticed a sharp pain on top of my right shoulder. I thought about and felt it out before categorizing my shoulder stabs as "pain to push through," and kept on. Even if they were in the "pain I should attend to" category, I was almost at the end of the race, so I think I would have pushed through it anyway. That's the kind of thinking that injures athletes, I guess.

With the last 4 miles of the marathon came a new and exaggerated energy. I started to encourage the people I passed, wave to fans on the sidelines, and I even made a couple of winning jokes. There was a lady on the side of the course handing out clear plastic cups with orange objects inside. My bike glided closer and I saw they were orange slices.

"I was excited because I thought those were Cheetos," I shouted as I passed.

Like before, my sense of humor was slacking. Even so, we both laughed at me like I made the joke of the year. Again, adapting to my audience.

I approached the end of the long road and the crowd began to thicken. There was a new energy in the air that I could tell something good was coming. I looked ahead and saw a giant, inflatable canopy and a cluster of fans in the distance that could only be the finish line. Strangers were standing behind gates, screaming loud, and waving green objects toward runners on the course. A smile spread across my face and I pushed my bike's handles harder than ever.

As I swam closer to the crowd, I began to feel the relief of the end coming around to smack me in the face. In marathons, this is usually the point where my ugly-relief-cry happens and I have to juggle trying to hide the ugly and push to the finish. With the intensity of the crowd as my cue, I felt my face wretch up and eyes water. Actually it's embarrassing and I hope I never see a picture of myself during that time. I know and I can feel how ugly my face is in those moments.

"Kristin Beale from Richmond, Virginia," I heard what I assumed to be the tiny man over the loud speaker. My race bib had a tracker on it so they could see and call out my information as I cross the finish line.

I rolled through the inflatable canopy and looked to my right at the race clock. I was overcome by relief and happiness, but mostly shock: four hours and three minutes. I beat my previous marathon time by 27 whole minutes. And the ugly-relief-cry began.

Four hours and 3 minutes later, we watched as our hero crossed the finish line. This was her third marathon in less than ideal weather, but she was feeling great. I jumped the fence (frowned upon) and hugged her tight. "I feel great, Dad. I'm not even tired." Yeah, right.

So, with the tireless spirit of a true competitor, Kristin was successful. Is it any wonder she'll walk again one day?

The moments following the finish line felt foreign to me. I received my medal from a happy stranger standing on the sideline, then rolled through the crowd to catch my Gatorade Recovery drink, hat, bag of pretzels, towel, and most notably my banana. I heard Dad's voice faintly singing from behind me.

"I am so proud of you," he walked into my vision and said. "Let me take this."

He snatched my post-marathon-swag from my lap so I could move my bike without my handles pushing it all to the ground.

"Are you cold?" Dad hovered over me and asked. "I got us passes to the VIP tent and it's heated. There's also food."

He was talking to my nodding head. My nodding, grateful head.

I floated into the VIP tent and Dad led the way to a table in front of a heater. He left me sitting alone until he returned with 2 Styrofoam platters of vegetable soup and a turkey sandwich. I ate the tasteless food while we watched a large television that showed a live broadcast of the finish line. The VIP tent is a luxury people have to pay extra money for, but we got in for free because Dad knows everyone, everywhere. That's called being a Beale.

The Shamrock Marathon was cold, but worth every second. My right shoulder took a beating and I busted my butt to finish a marathon with no training, but it was worth it. Every strain and every exertion I had to endure was worth it. I beat my marathon time by 27 minutes. It was all worth it.

Friday, August 28 (10 years after injury)
– An entry from Dad's CaringBridge journal.

> *Love bears all things, believes all things, hopes all things, endures all things.*

Our focus as a family is looking forward. While things of the past are crucial to the path of the future, no one looking backwards can see to go forward.

Kristin's condition resulted in loss of feeling below the naval. This obviously affects a lot of things we take for granted. This is a marathon, not a sprint. Speaking of marathons, Kristin has completed 7 so far on her handcycle. Her favorites are the Marine Corps marathon, which is one of the most grueling, and the Shamrock Marathon in Va. Beach. She continues to wait and train at the very last minute. Oh, to be young. God has blessed our family in so many ways and there is a lesson in all of this.

My mantra is "It can always be worse" when seemingly insurmountable challenges come our way. There's a lot of truth in that and it most certainly prepares us for the worst. I could fill a book or talk for hours on this. I thank God for giving us Kristin as a witness to what can be achieved through faith.

Many years ago in 2005, our lives changed. Kristin continues to call it a blessing, but we continue to view it as something entirely different. We all realize that, in spite of what happened, we are still blessed. Our family dynamic changed permanently and, to this day, we sometimes have difficulty managing those changes. Many families will break apart for a host of reasons when tragedy strikes. We are blessed.

"Time heals all wounds."

We've all heard that. I'm here to say that the wound has not healed so far, but the intensity of the wound has lessened. This is all attributable to the grace that God gives us to endure all things and the success of the monumental hurdles that Kristin has leaped in her young life. We watch Kristin struggle daily with what she considers "small things" but, from the outside looking in, all I can think is "How does she deal with that every *day?" Yet another testimony to a very big heart that takes on anything thrown her way and shrugs it off while thinking "Is that all you got? Bring it."*

The silver lining of any challenge in life is that they create stories. The stories illustrate for those that will never face the difficulties, but they also let you look behind the curtain. Looking back there can be scary, but it can also be uplifting. Kristin has done that for us.

CHAPTER 24

Greater Things

I fall asleep and wake up to this disability every day of my life. Everything I do and every interaction I have is a product of how people accept and accommodate my special condition, reflected in both how they perceive me and whether they choose to accommodate me. My wheelchair makes it impossible to hide my dissimilarity in ways most disabled people are able; I have no choice but to deal with judgment and unacceptance on a daily basis. I feel locked inside of a damaged body and I can't find a way out.

My struggle for normalcy in my appearance, interactions, and lifestyle is never-ending. My body has been broken and it has not able to snap back into the circumstance of before my accident. Not only can I not walk or have normal feeling below my injury level, I'm also unable to sit comfortably in a wheelchair, maneuver into and out of public with ease, interact equally with my peers, and a never-ending list of set-backs. A spinal cord injury requires me to live inside the stigma of physical difference and alongside an invisible legion of intense and unpredictable side effects. People feel bad for me because I can't walk, but that's the least of my problems.

I don't think I'll ever get answers to my long list of questions and I know I'll never understand the reasons for all the hurt in my life. But that's just how life is. Before I turned 15 years old, I had already faced more tragedy and was expected to handle it with more maturity than most of my adult peers. My focus switched from sports practice and attractive boys, to wiggling my toes and learning to put on pants independently. The majority of my years in high school are a blur of memories of lost friendships, special accommodations, and incontinence.

I miss the days I could play on a normal sports team and I want so badly to be able to stand up and dance with my father at my wedding. I want people to treat me equally and it's not fair for them to assume my inability. I don't want people to feel uncomfortable around me and I don't want to feel obligated to break ice by talking about my accident with every new person. I'm tired of hearing apologies for my situation and I'm frustrated with being made an object of pity. It's not fair. More than I want to walk, I want people to love and accept me for the person I am at this point in my life: a temporarily disabled woman.

There's an unreasonable amount of sadness and rejection laced into my story of a spinal cord injury at age 14. I would like to say I'm thankful for every hardship that has been thrown at me but, honestly, I'm not. There's a long list of things that broke me down in places I felt were already broken, and a few times I thought I was going to give up. I don't think I'll ever understand a reason for that. The internal battle against my circumstance is daily and unrelenting. I'm frustrated with my nerves for not responding to my brain; I'm frustrated with God for continuing to let bad things happen to me; and I'm frustrated with my peers for running away when I needed them most.

But greater things are coming.

I'm thankful for the timing of my accident. My story started when I was in high school – a time I was able to focus on myself. After I left the hospital I was able to leave school to travel across the country, I came home to a loving family and community that accommodated my freshly-ignited rehabilitative goals, and I was able to fill my life with people who will ultimately help guide me closer to my goal of independently walking.

God worked everything out perfectly.

But now I grow up. Immediately following graduation I got a job at the front desk of the YMCA, then to a law firm, then to a mortgage company. I built my first house, have my own dog, a beautiful boyfriend, and can live independently. My life is nothing what I planned it to be. But that's the cool part: God shook me up then put me back together again. Slowly, on His own time and not without struggles, but I landed on my feet. My wheels, if we're being technical.

I've said it for years: my accident is the best thing that has happened to me. With reason, people have trouble believing that becoming paralyzed is a highlight, but it definitely is. The people I've met, places I've traveled, and opportunities I've had since my accident are irreplaceable and act as reminders of how fortunate I am and how bad I actually don't have it. If a cup of Jell-O falls on the floor, you don't stand there and try to figure out why it fell – you clean it up before it stains the rug. Sometimes, most of the time, we don't know why frustrating or difficult or painful things happen to us. We just deal with it and try to get our lives as close to "normal" as we can. If you're smart, you'll let those bad things happen and search for the positive parts. There are always positive parts. Even in the most traumatic, awful situations, there are positive parts. You just have to search.

Have you ever heard anyone say "God doesn't give you more than you can handle?" Well that isn't true. He definitely does. But here's the thing: He'll help us handle it. I promise you that's the only reason I can handle myself right now. I had some serious help.

Disability changed my life in a way I never could have imagined I could handle; I've had to deal with distress, confusion, isolation, and frustration more than any person should be required. My journey is long, difficult, and deep-rooted, but it has shaped my interests, improved my interactions, and tested my psyche in ways I would have never asked, but am exceedingly thankful for. My situation and rehabilitation give me something to work hard for. It gives me a chance to focus my mind and eventually see or feel a product of it. As long as I continue to work toward a normally-functioning body, I'm headed toward an uphill victory. I'm headed toward greater things.

This is just the beginning of my story.

Morgan James
Speakers Group

We connect Morgan James published authors with live and online events and audiences whom will benefit from their expertise.